Dean

Daring to Live Like My Brother with Down Syndrome

JONATHAN ADCOCK

DEDICATION

To my brother. My best friend. The best person I've ever known.
Today is another day closer to seeing you again.

CONTENTS

1

EVERYONE'S HERO

My brother Dean is a legend.

He's that larger-than-life-itself kind of guy, despite the fact that he stood at just 5'3" (or, as he would point out, 5'4" in basketball shoes).

He was the kind of guy who quickly made friends with everyone he met, but he also made each person he talked to feel like they were the most important person in the world.

He was good at sports, the starting point guard on his basketball team and quarterback for his football team. The cheerleaders knew and loved him, as did everyone in the crowd.

He could dance with the best, with range from Usher to Michael Jackson to The Temptations and Franki Valli. He shined brightest in the spotlight, though he cared just as much about sharing it with those he loved the most.

He was brave. He was strong. He was patient. He was kind.

He was my hero.

Dean Adcock was more than a brother to me, more than a son to my parents, and more than a friend to those who knew him. He was a light to everyone he encountered and a model for how to love people and how to live life with pure joy and appreciation.

Dean was born with a limitation; one that would stump his mental and physical development as compared to his peers. He had Trisomy 21, better known as Down syndrome.

Born in 1984, having Down syndrome meant that Dean would develop more slowly than other kids his age. Because of that, he would simply not be afforded the same opportunities and rite-of-passage moments most of us look back on as some of the most formative moments of our lives.

He never had a driver's license (which if you ever saw him play a driving video game, you would say this was a good thing). He never married (he was too much of a ladies' man for that anyway). He never had a full-time job. He never lived in his own place.

Dean's life with Down syndrome included struggling with things we take for granted. Math skills always eluded him. He needed help with his reading comprehension and, when he was younger, his speech. He was slower to develop his muscle tone and finer motor skills. Even his immune system didn't protect him as well as a "normal" person's would.

But Dean's life was never built around things he couldn't do. Dean's disability was, in my opinion, one of his greatest strengths. Dean may have had Down syndrome, but he was also the most joyful, pure-hearted person I have ever known. He had a special outlook on life, one that always saw the good in others, found new ways to accomplish things, and was never defeated by any obstacle placed before him.

Down syndrome didn't disable Dean; it made him different. In the best way possible.

Dean forged a new path for himself and defied all odds given to my parents when he was born. His social skills far exceeded anyone in our family (so did his dance moves). His passion for life inspired everyone he met. His love for other people was pure and unconditional.

It's hard for me to speculate what Dean's life would have been like had he not had Down syndrome. But I don't have to. I can rest assured knowing that Dean didn't mind it. As he told us one day, unprompted, "I love my life."

That's more than a lot of us can say for ourselves.

So how did Dean get there? How did he go from a doctor saying, "Your son has facial features that make us believe he has Trisomy 21," to, "Dean was one of the most incredible people I've ever known"?

I have to tell you—it's a pretty incredible story.

Part of my mission in life is to tell that story. And that's what this book is.

As Dean's brother (he'd never call me his "little" brother; only his "younger, taller" brother), I've had the best seat in the house to watch him grow and transform and transcend any perceived limitations as he became the one-of-a-kind man everyone knew him to be.

I've unashamedly ridden his coattails to some of coolest experiences of either of our lives, from watching Dean dance onstage in front of hundreds of his friends to being selected by our beloved Carolina Panthers to attend Super Bowl LII.

And along the way, I've learned more from Dean than I could have ever taught him.

He taught me the value of gratitude by appreciating everything and everyone in his life. He showed me what it looks like to relish the moment, to smile and laugh and hug somebody, and to make the most of any situation. He loved people unconditionally and naturally understood that each person on this planet carries his or her own unique, intrinsic value.

Dean lived more in thirty-three years than most of us will be able to achieve in all of our lifetimes combined.

I often think of the times Dean would whimsically say

things like, "Jon, one day I get my own TV show. I call it, 'Everybody Loves Dean'."

He's right. Everybody loved him.

I always dreaded the day that Dean would no longer be with us. The thought would cross my mind several times over the years, each thought as sudden as it was unwelcome. I'd get physically sick to my stomach and think to myself, "No, I never want to be without Dean."

But actually living in this reality, and being forced to go on without Dean, hurts so much more than I could have ever imagined.

I miss his daily phone calls, all of which started the same: "Hi Jon, how you doing? I just call to say I love you."

I miss his smile, his hugs, and his insatiable appetite for anything related to the things he loved. He would update me daily on the Carolina Panthers and Charlotte Hornets. And no matter what was going on in the world, I knew I could walk into his bedroom and find him dancing and singing to his favorite music.

My world is not nearly as bright without his light shining in it.

That's why I started writing. This process is therapeutic for me. I find my greatest joy lately when I'm telling Dean's story. I love laughing at some of the things he used to do or say, I love marveling at the way he danced, and I love the pride that comes with knowing I got to be such a special part of such a special person's life.

The more I tell his story, the more I see how bright his light truly was, and the more I want to share that light with the world.

So, one day, I took a day off of work to try to clear my head and regain some sense of clarity in my heart and mind. And while sorting through the muck and mess of my own grief, this book sprung to life.

I thought, I don't just need to write for myself anymore. I need to give this—to give Dean—to the world.

I've always believed, "If only everyone knew Dean or had someone like Dean in their lives, the world would be a much better place."

So here we go.

Even if no one reads this book besides my wife and my parents (although too many people loved Dean to believe that's even possible), I owe this to him. I'd like to imagine that Dean would hold this book in his hands, see his handwriting on the cover, and exclaim, "Oh, cool! I love it!"

Then, Dean would give me the biggest hug you'd ever get from someone standing five-foot-three.

Though his absence has inevitably brought me grief and sadness, his memory will always bring me joy. The way Dean lived his life inspires me to be a better person. Writing about him has been such a healing experience for me.

I pray that this book will not only allow you to get to know Dean, but will leave you with a clearer picture of pure joy and how to access it like he did.

This is my brother. This is Dean. This is my hero. And by the end of this, he might just be your hero too.

2

"JON SAID D WORD!"

The year was 1994. It was a good year—the United States hosted the World Cup, Michael Jordan tried his hand at baseball, and Forrest Gump taught us all that, "Life was like a box of chocolates; you never know what you're gonna get."

I would say that growing up with Dean, you never knew what you were gonna get either.

Yes, he was fun, outgoing, and always playing sports. But he was also quite mischievous. That's something I believe runs in the Adcock family DNA—a "creative" approach to misbehaving.

There was never a dull moment with young Dean. He went to elementary school at Devonshire Elementary on the east side of Charlotte, NC, where he and his best friends had a knack for getting into trouble.

One day, my dad had to be called to come pick Dean up from school because he had gotten upset and flipped over a desk in the middle of class. When asked why he did such a thing, Dean replied, "Because Matt said I farted!"

You can't make this stuff up.

We also had a rule in our house that whenever Dean and I went anywhere as kids, if one of us got into trouble, then both of us would be in trouble when we got home. I hated that rule, primarily because it meant I had the task of keeping my creatively-mischievous brother out of trouble.

Mind you, Dean never was outright deviant; just creative. He specifically loved to aggravate our grandmother, Ruth Adcock. She was a devout Southern Baptist who shared Dean's love for Elvis Presley (although she would only listen to his Gospel records, saying, "He really wasted his talent not singing for the Lord!"). She was not fond of some of Dean's antics, and Dean thought it was hilarious to get underneath her skin.

If she said, "Dean, don't touch that," Dean would, naturally, touch it immediately. With one finger. And a devilish grin.

If she said, "Dean, don't listen to that trashy music," Dean would ever-so-slightly turn up the volume.

One time at one of her favorite fish camp restaurants (you might have to be Southern to understand that this was just a buffet of fried fish), she said, "Dean, why'd you eat that nasty, greasy hushpuppy?" (Again, Southern thing.)

Dean snapped back, with his mouth still full, "Because it's good!"

I would beg Dean, "Come on, man, don't get us in trouble today!"

Dean would reassure me, "I not Jon, I not. I'm good today."

Then, ten minutes later, when my grandmother asked Dean to get her handicap parking pass out of the glove compartment so she could park up-front at Eastland Mall, Dean scoffed:

"Why? You not handicapped!"

I shook my head in the backseat of her 1980-something Honda. Once we got home, we were getting a butt whooping.

It never seemed to bother Dean though. When it came to spankings, I typically went first, and he was last on the card as The Main Event. But Dean was also the master of turning on the waterworks at the right time, getting so worked up and afraid before the spanking even took place that he would either get off without the spanking, or with a lesser sentence, like no video games for a few hours.

I knew it was coming, and I never thought it was fair. After all, Dean would be singing and dancing to his favorite music again before my backside stopped stinging.

But none of that compared to the ways he used to scheme to get his younger brother into trouble. He saved his best, most clever tricks for me.

On this quiet, early-1990's evening, Dean and I were watching the movie "Beethoven" on VHS. We were just hanging out, talking, playing, and keeping up with our favorite Saint Bernard pup.

In that movie, Ted, the nerdy, glasses-wearing son in Beethoven's family, got picked on quite a bit. The bullies at school were quick to tease him, pour milk cartons on his head, and call him a "dork" throughout the movie.

Stay with me here.

Sometime towards the end of the movie, Dean was getting restless. He was talking a lot—something he never grew out of—and clearly disturbing my attempt to watch and see what happens to Beethoven.

To this day, I cannot remember what question he asked me, but I felt like it was a dumb question that he already knew the answer to because my response was simply:

"Duh, you dork!"

(That's one of the most '90's things I may have ever said, by the way.)

As soon as I said it, Dean got that grin on his face. The

kind that told you he had an idea, and it wasn't going to be anything good for me.

He was sitting cross-legged on the floor, right by the bedroom door, when he suddenly leapt to his feet, burst through the door and sprinted down the hallway to the top of the stairs.

"Mom! Dad! Jon said D word! Jon said D word!"

Uh-oh.

In our house, cussing meant one thing: Washing your mouth out with soap. Dean knew it, and he wanted to see me be the first to take the punishment for it.

So naturally, I knew what the real "D word" was (not because we heard it from our parents or anything like that) and I immediately jumped into action to defend my name (and taste buds).

"No I didn't! I swear! I didn't! He's lying!"

Dean, laughing all the way down the stairs, with me in pursuit, "Yes he did! Jon said D word!"

And before I could explain to my parents that I just spent the last hour becoming well-versed on the word "dork" through the movie Beethoven, I was being ushered into the downstairs bathroom.

There it was—the generic, orange, antibacterial hand-soap from Food Lion. I knew in that moment that washing my hands would never be the same.

I had to take 3-4 generous pumps of that God-forsaken soap onto my tongue and hold it in my mouth for what felt like an eternity (it was probably only seconds).

Then, while swishing it around in my mouth and waiting for the word to spit it out, there was Dean. He hung an arm on the side of the door frame, laughing so hard his aviator-style eyeglasses were fogging up.

The truth meant nothing at that point. Dean had won.

It was years later, when I was in high school, that I finally told my parents the truth of what happened that fateful evening. I explained to them everything, from Beethoven to Dean running down the hall to the years of wondering whether or not "dork" really was the infamous "D word".

And then, in that moment, I finally got what I waited over a decade to hear:

"Dean, is that true? Did you do that to your brother?"

Dean chuckled.

"Yes, I did."

"Why did you do it, Dean?"

Still laughing, Dean answered, "I don't know. I sorry Jon. That's in the past."

Then he gave me the biggest Dean hug you could

imagine.

I didn't know whether I should trust the hug, honestly. Dean was still Dean, after all, and he was capable of getting me into trouble at any moment.

But I loved it.

I loved it because in reality, it was hilarious. He pulled off a trick far too clever for what his young mind was supposed to be capable of. He knew exactly what he was doing and what was going to happen to me when he did. He knew that "dork" wasn't the real "D-word" and he also knew that it didn't matter; I was going to get in trouble anyway.

Now, Dean had officially owned up to his conniving ways and finally admitted that he had scarred me to the point of avoiding a particular type of hand soap for my entire life, all for a quick laugh.

And then, after the hug, Dean looked up at me (I had long-since surpassed him in height), and he said one of his favorite go-to phrases:

"We still brothers, Jon?"

"Absolutely, Dean. Brothers forever."

3

MAKING HIS OWN WAY

Recently, my Dad said to me, "One thing I worried about when Dean was born was, 'How would people treat him?'"

I'm sure he was worried about how mean people can be to each other, especially to those different than them. Thankfully, Dean didn't have to worry much about that.

Dean was a beacon of joy. He had this magnetic presence about him that drew you in and made you smile, no matter what.

Perhaps it was his smile, his eyes beaming and his lips curling upwards as if they were trying to reach his ears. Maybe it was his dance moves, the kind of spins and dips and leg kicks that draw a crowd every time. Or maybe it was his charm, set off with a simple, "Hi, how you doing? Awesome!"

But whatever "it" was, Dean had it. He never had an issue making friends, and he certainly never had any enemies.

Dean's best friend growing up was a young man named Matt Price. Their teachers and summer camp counselors called him and Dean, "Pete and Repeat."

The two were inseparable from the age of two, meeting in a developmental center and sticking together all the way into high school.

Dean and Matt both had Down syndrome, and both shared a knack for mischief.

Once, on a high school field trip to the newly-opened Concord Mills Mall, Matt and Dean were separated from their classmates for quite some time. Panicked, his teachers enlisted the help of the mall's security officers to track them down.

And, of course, they found Dean and Matt sitting on a bench outside of one of the stores, with newspapers conveniently opened up to cover their faces. (I've always wondered, "Where did they get the newspapers?!")

Clever as they were, I'm sure it was the short legs and matching wide-width New Balances that gave them away. When asked why they ran away, they sheepishly grinned at each other.

"Dean, Matt... Were you looking for girls?"

"Yes."

They were kindred spirits.

While Dean was in high school though, he had a knack for breaking away from the crowd like this. Always too cool for everything around him, Dean always tried to make his own path.

If he was supposed to walk in a straight line, he hovered over to the side. If asked to wear a specific t-shirt for a school function, he'd wear a Mark McGwire baseball jersey over it.

But more than anything, Dean wanted to fit in with the "regular" students.

Dean always wrestled with this notion that he was different from other people his age. By the time he was a teenager, he had begun to see his friends get their drivers licenses, drive their first cars, find their first girlfriends and boyfriends, and explore the possibility of going to college.

He would say things to me like, "Jon, I not drive like my friends. I not go to college like my friends. Why?"

This was long before I knew of the many programs and opportunities available to young adults with special needs—I was five years younger than Dean, mind you—so I didn't know how to respond.

I would try to remind him that he wasn't just different; he was special. That no matter what he could or couldn't do, he was awesome in his own right.

I don't know how much of that truly got through to him, but he walked with the swagger of someone who knew he was special.

In fact, it got him in trouble sometimes. He would begin to lag behind the rest of his classmates as they walked through the school, trying his best to be seen or associated with him when the "cool kids" walked by.

Dean was very fortunate from elementary to middle to high school to have excellent teachers. They embraced Dean's desire to be different and allowed him to dream. His high school teachers even enrolled him in a homeroom full of students without disabilities. Although Dean didn't have the capacity to keep up academically with those students, just a few minutes a day in the same class as them was enough to make him feel like the King of the school.

And oh, did he ever make himself King of East Mecklenburg High School.

Marshall Glenn, the star quarterback of the school football team, and one of the top college football prospects in the state at the time, was a member of the East Meck "Dream Team", a group of student-athletes who committed to stay drug and alcohol-free. Part of their team's activities included serving as "Peer Tutors" in Dean's special-needs class.

An avid football fan (that's putting it lightly), Dean loved Marshall immediately. And Marshall made sure to take care of Dean. That meant on Fridays in the Fall, when the East Meck football team held their "Spirit March" through the hallways to the beat of the school drumline (it was their version of a pep rally), they would be sure to pass Dean's classroom. Once, Marshall stopped the entire procession just to single Dean out, high-five him, and introduce him to the other players.

Dean was in.

The "Dream Team" hosted Valentine's Day dances for the Special Education classes—Dean won "King" of the dance two years in a row. A local public-access television program filmed a story on Marshall and the "Dream Team", which of course included plenty of close-ups of Dean.

Soon, Dean would no longer be eating lunch with his class; he'd be sitting with Marshall and the football players.

And the cheerleaders.

Trust me, nothing made Dean smile wider or blush harder than getting a hug from one of the cheerleaders.

In Charlotte-Mecklenburg Schools, Dean was allowed to attend high-school all the way to age 21. Dean saw many of his football and cheerleading buddies come and go, but the coaches and "Dream Team" athletes made sure to keep Dean's traditions alive.

One season, Dean even got to spend each home game on the sideline as the East Meck Eagles' official Water Boy. Forget high-fives in the hallway; Dean was practically in the huddle.

But by that point, East Meck's football team was no longer a top-three team in the area, so Dean spent as much time showing his displeasure for his team's mistakes as he did hydrating them during timeouts.

But win or lose, Dean's mission was accomplished. His two worlds were no longer separated by "regular" and "different" students. It was all intertwined—even his best friend and partner-in-crime Matt Price would feel the love from the school's jocks and "cool kids".

I know it's not normal for teenage kids to treat someone like Dean with respect and adoration. Some kids can be cruel in how they mock and ridicule people with disabilities. And I think that's the fear my Dad had as Dean grew up, a fear any parent of a child with disabilities would reasonably have.

But Dean didn't just help change the norm for how people like him were treated in his school; he changed the way those teachers and students saw themselves too.

Dean's high school teacher, Mrs. Hanson, who was his all-time favorite teacher, had this to say about Dean:

"One of my favorite memories was when I was invited to a party at Dean's house. I took my little girls with me—they were still in elementary school at the time. Dean greeted us at the door and was so excited to see us… They just met Dean and he was now their friend. Once you met Dean, you loved him, but he loved you more. Dean loved my girls. But more than that, it was this party that developed the passion and compassion that my girls have for people with disabilities. They have volunteered for Special Olympics for many years, not only here in the United States but also in Guam and Australia. My daughter Haley even played on a unified flag football team with Dean and competed at the University of Maryland in 2012. Their love for Special Olympics was all because of the friendship with Dean that was born out of a party.

Dean easily made friends everywhere he went. But when his friend Marshall, the quarterback, stopped the entire Spirit March to introduce Dean, everything was silent for a minute. But Marshall introduced Dean as his friend and Dean was absolutely thrilled. I just stood there in amazement with tears in my eyes. The Spirit March continued on and Dean's day was made. I imagine when we get to Heaven, Dean will meet us with a Spirit March of his own, and he will make sure to stop to introduce us all to his friends."

Dean may not have had the traditional high school experiences that shaped many of our lives, and that's fine. He was too busy making his own experiences—and making everyone else's that much better.

4

"DON'T LOOK AT ME!

I'M NOT DOING IT!"

In the Fall of 2006, Dean was in the midst of a career year as quarterback of the Challenger Flag Football League. His lefty toss was matched only by his leadership in the huddle.

I believe this was his favorite season of all-time because he was paired up with some of his best friends.

Justin, who had known Dean since they were only two years old, Ben, who went to high school with Dean, and Caleb, who lived next door, all lined up on the same squad that Fall.

On the field, they would draw up fancy reverse passes and option runs that gave each of them a chance to score. And while you're at it, why not come up with a few touchdown dances that, if we had cameras, would have easily made the SportsCenter Top 10 countdown?

But off the field, these best friends were even more dynamic.

Dean had more friends than I could count, but these were his best buds. Each of the guys in their friend group were equally girl-crazy; they would laugh about wanting to go to Hooters for their birthday (for the wings, of course).

Or if we were driving down the highway and passed an adult night club, one of them would snicker and say, "What is that? I want to go there!"

They would go to concerts together—Justin is a huge country music fan and easily got Dean to wear a cowboy hat and strum a guitar as if he were Kenny Chesney. They would all go to games together, as each of them were diehard sports fans. And when they weren't watching sports together, they were playing every sport they could together, from their Challenger Flag Football team to Special Olympics softball and bowling.

Ben is also a tremendous swimmer; Dean made sure to stay in the shallow end.

Regardless of where they were, what they were doing, or what kind of trouble they were dreaming of getting into together, they knew how to look out for one another.

For example, one of the guys in the group tended to get lost in public places, so whenever he needed to go to the bathroom at a restaurant, one of the other guys would immediately say, "I'll take you," to make sure he got back safely.

If one didn't know how to tie their shoes or had difficulty buckling his belt, one of them would jump in to help. There was no teasing or hesitation on any of their parts—they just had each other's backs. Every time.

That's why this fateful day in the Fall of 2006 stands out so clearly to me.

One of Dean's friends rode home with Dean and me after their flag football game. His parents were headed somewhere for the afternoon and would pick him up that evening. Coincidentally, my parents were also gone for the afternoon, so it was just Dean, his friend, and me at our house for a few hours.

He and Dean went straight to Dean's room to play video games. Dean, in his usual fashion, clicked on his stereo as soon as he entered the room and skimmed through a Jackson 5 CD until he found the song, "ABC."

"Jackson 5 again?" Dean's friend asked.

"Yeah! I love Michael Jackson. And Tito and Jermaine too." Dean replied, already two-stepping to the beat.

I headed into my bedroom and shut the door, thinking this was the perfect time to catch up on some homework.

Just over an hour later, there was a sudden knock on my bedroom door. It wasn't a polite knock either. It was a police-sounding knock; the kind that makes your heart jump up to the top of your throat.

"Jon! He had a accident!" Dean shouted.

Uh-oh.

I swung the door open.

"What kind of accident?"

"I don't know," Dean shook his head. "Just come here."

Dean started down the hallway shaking his head, as if to say, "You're not going to believe this."

He stopped in front of the bathroom door. The light was on and I could hear the exhaust fan buzzing from inside.

"In there, Jon."

I tapped on the door gently.

"Are you okay in there?" I asked.

No response.

"I'm going to open the door. Is that okay?"

"Okay…" I finally heard from inside the bathroom.

As I cracked the door open, there was Dean's friend, standing in front of the toilet with his pants pulled down to his ankles. A torn piece of toilet paper (we always bought the cheap stuff) was stuck to his hand.

And poop was everywhere.

His hands. His legs. The floor. The toilet seat.

Everywhere.

"I sorry…." Came from the bathroom as Dean's friend ducked his head in shame and embarrassment.

It was clear he was going to need a lot of help to get cleaned up.

Before I said anything, I looked at Dean.

"Don't look at me! I'm not doing it!" Dean threw his hands up and began to back away.

I don't know what Dean could smell more in that moment—his friend's accident or my fear.

I swear to you that my life flashed before my eyes in an instant.

I saw all the moments where I was squeamish towards vomit, bowel movements, blood, and other bodily fluids. I felt my gag reflex not just kicking in, but assaulting my reflexes.

I looked at Dean's friend again and wondered, "Well… How long before his parents get here again?"

No. I couldn't. I didn't want to. But my goodness, I had

no choice.

For the next five to ten minutes, Dean's friend and I got closer than I ever wanted to be.

I got him cleaned up and into some clean clothes. I restored our bathroom to clean and working order. I sprayed about a pint of air freshener into that bathroom.

Most teenage or early-twenties-aged guys would never let their friends live that down. Not the accident, not the clean-up, nothing.

But thankfully for Dean's friend and me, we told his parents what happened and never spoke of it again.

I preferred acting like that never happened anyway.

But here we are, in a book that will live on forever, inviting you into my worst nightmare.

I thought the whole experience was indicative of how Dean and his friends operated. Yes, they make mistakes and have accidents, including some they had no control over. But there was never any judgment or condescension from it at all. They just took care of each other and moved on.

Inclusivity was effortless for Dean and his friends. They loved and accepted each other unconditionally.

Earlier that day, their group of friends took turns supporting the athletes in powered wheelchairs during their flag football game.

For example, one young man had cerebral palsy and was in a wheelchair, but didn't have the motor functions to actually catch a football. Dean, as the quarterback, would snap the ball, drop back, and throw it to a volunteer standing next to him. Justin, Ben, Caleb, and all of Dean's friends and teammates, would either become blockers clearing a path for the young man's chair, or run to the opposite side of the field to take their defender as far away from the ball as possible.

Again, this was never coached; it was something they instinctively knew to do. It was someone else's time to shine and they were determined to make it happen for them.

And I'm forever grateful for so many people who did the same for him.

Dean served as the bat boy for every Little League Baseball team I was ever on, and my teammates and coaches always looked out for him.

Once, an umpire, who seemed to have an issue with people having fun, told Dean he could not participate in that game unless he wore a helmet at all times. Dean didn't have a helmet, but our coach immediately dug one out of one of our players' bags and handed it to Dean.

That same coach would end every practice with Dean getting a chance to bat as if he were in an actual game (with a helmet on, of course). As soon as he hit the ball, every kid on the team would act as if we were making the play, but either drop the ball, throw the ball away, or stumble goofily while Dean made his way around the bases.

After a few wayward throws and feigned goof-ups in the field, Dean would cross home plate for an inside-the-park home run. A few of us would rush Dean with hugs and high fives while the rest of us dramatically fell to the turf as if we'd just blown the biggest game of our careers.

Dean was part of the team. He was included. But more than that, my teammates became Dean's friends.

Friends don't let differences, disabilities, or even bathroom accidents drive them apart. Friends find ways to make each other heroes. And Dean was a hero in that moment.

What would the world look like if such inclusivity was second-nature? What if we didn't criticize our differences, but celebrated them? What if we didn't remind people of their mistakes, but helped them get cleaned up instead? What if instead of trying to strike everyone out (metaphorically speaking), we made sure everyone got their chance to hit a home run?

I was lucky enough to get a glimpse of what that was like inside of Dean's world. And it was beautiful.

5

"Go Dean! Go Dean! Go Dean!"

There he was again, in his element.

The bass thumping through the walls.
The people clapping.
Chanting his name.
The spotlight shining bright.

Directly on Dean.

I could pinpoint this exact scene at least three times in my brother Dean's life. It was at "Night to Shine", an event hosted at our church, put on by the Tim Tebow Foundation as a prom for people with special needs.

The premise of the night was simple—to make these young men and women feel like Kings and Queens, if only for a night.

Dean relished his moment.

Truthfully, he didn't just relish this moment; he relished every moment of his thirty-three years on Earth. He was grateful, attentive, and ever-present in any given moment.

But especially this one.

The song "OMG" by Usher pumped through the auditorium, reverberating off the walls and vaulted ceiling. A few hundred people with special needs cheered and sang along. They were each decked out in their finest suits, dresses, blazers, and, most importantly, their dancing shoes.

Some swayed back-and-forth to the beat. Others partnered up and took turns twirling each other in circles. But there, onstage, singled-out, in front of everybody, flawlessly executing each of Usher's dance moves from the "OMG" music video:

Dean.

I'll have to admit, dancing onstage in front of other people is my worst nightmare. But it was Dean's dream-come-true.

He floated momentarily from left-to-right, opening his suit jacket with one hand, and allowing the other to flutter out towards the crowd. I can only guess he was pointing to a girl. He came back to center, bringing both arms up to form an "O" shape, rotating the letter in step with Usher's "o-o-o-o-o-o"s. Then, the beat drops, and Dean goes into a full-blown dance break.

The crowd went wild.

I was there, standing a few feet from the lip of the stage, just far enough back from the crowd to not have to dance (because let's be honest, the people who dance up front are the best dancers, and I wasn't ready for that life). I couldn't help but laugh.

"That's my brother!" I thought, "But with those moves, I don't know if we're really even related."

My brother lived for the limelight and had a knack for finding it. He stretched his "fifteen minutes of fame" into a lifetime of cheers, high-fives, and celebrations. This was all perfectly fine with me and my family, for we all preferred to be the ones in the background, cheering on those in the spotlight. It made it easy for us to cherish these memories; the "only-Dean-could-pull-this-off" types of moments that he made look easy.

For all of his accolades, from winning gold medals in the Special Olympics to playing one-on-one basketball with Charlotte Hornets' legend Muggsy Bogues, to getting selected to attend the Super Bowl by our beloved Carolina Panthers, dancing onstage in front of his friends might have been Dean's favorite.

Dean counted down the days every year to many of his favorite events—birthdays, Christmas, summer camp, the NFL Draft—but the three "Night to Shine" events he got to attend were the crème de la crème for him.

His very first "Night to Shine" was extra-special. This

annual event, spearheaded by the Tim Tebow Foundation, takes place on one night each year, with churches and organizations across multiple countries hosting the event in their communities.

It was the very first one put on in Charlotte, and hosted by the church that my wife Bekah and I work at, Elevation Church. We went all-out, as we do with all of our events, especially the ones that get to celebrate people as special as Dean and his friends. Our church has a reputation for making these kinds of events excellent, so much so that Tim Tebow himself scheduled our event as the first of his many stops that night across the United States.

So, in true Dean fashion, my brother found himself in the middle of an opportunity of a lifetime. Though his team mentioned that his stay would be just a few minutes, Tim Tebow stayed at our dance for over an hour. And somewhere in that time frame, I walked towards the dance floor only to find a mob of people doing "The Wobble" near the front of the stage—and right there in the thick of it, dancing next to Tim Tebow, was Dean.

That wasn't all, either. A photo of Tim Tebow walking down the red carpet with Cat, Dean's very special friend (not girlfriend, per his insistence, but we all knew the truth), wound up circulating all the way to People Magazine.

And of course, right behind Cat, with a big smile on his face, was Dean. In People Magazine.

You can't make this stuff up.

The glitz and glamor of that "Night to Shine" experience certainly appealed to Dean. After seeing his face in a magazine on the newsstand at the grocery store, Dean would very matter-of-factly say, "I famous again, Jon!"

But that wasn't the reason he counted down. He circled the calendar for "Night to Shine" because he knew he would get to dance his heart out with all of his friends. In his eyes, very few things in the world could compare to that.

I believe in large part that Dean loved dancing so much because it brought out some of the truest parts of himself. He never articulated it this way, but watching him, I always believed that when he got on the dance floor, he was always two things that most of us only dream of being:

Fearless and free.

Dean knew no shame when it came to living in the spotlight. Where I might clam up and become paralyzed by the thought of what others may be thinking, judging, or laughing at me for, Dean stepped up and owned the moment.

He was especially confident in his dancing, but it really didn't matter what Dean was doing. He was unapologetically himself at all times, never putting on a facade to impress anyone. Granted, you don't have to worry about impressing people when you can dance like Usher. Or Michael Jackson. Or The Temptations.

But when the music came on, it didn't matter if he was dancing next to Tim Tebow or by himself pushing the vacuum cleaner at home on a Thursday afternoon. He gave it his all. He had fun. And he didn't lose an ounce of sweat to insecurity, worry, or self-doubt.

The way Dean danced was symbolic of the way he lived his life. He moved through his world with a smooth, effortless sense of confidence. He changed the temperature of a room just by walking into it and flashing his smile. He made you feel like the most important person in the room whenever he talked to you, hugged you, and asked you how you were doing.

But he did it with a purity that let you know he wasn't looking for attention or notoriety. Don't get me wrong—if there's anyone who wanted to shine in the spotlight, it was Dean. But he didn't need it.

He danced because he loved to dance. He smiled because he was genuinely happy. And he sang because there was too much joy in his heart to keep it all to himself.

Dean was Dean. There was no one else quite like him and I'm convinced there may never be again.

And the Dean I saw onstage in front of hundreds of people was the same Dean that I saw every single day. Pure. Passionate. Fun. Talented. And free.

6

JUST BRAVE ENOUGH

The Intimidator.

Dean and I stared up at the twisted steel, winding back-and-forth, up-and-down, and peaking at a height 232 feet from the ground.

"The Intimidator" lived up to its name.

"Dean, you sure you want to do this?"

"I don't know, Jon."

"Come on man, we got this."

At the time, this was the newest roller-coaster at Carowinds, a theme park nestled between a pair of major highways and straddling the North and South Carolina borders.

To Dean and me, this place was pure fun. We loved the rides, the laughter, the nearly-impossible carnival games, and the ice cream cones that saved us from the Carolina summer heat.

There was only one small hindrance: Dean was terrified of heights.

This wasn't just the kind of "afraid of heights" that meant you got nervous and your heart pounded looking out of the window of a tall building. This was the full-body-paralysis kind, the type of fear that shut everything down as if someone had just hit Control + Alt + Delete on your entire nervous system.

Maybe roller-coasters weren't the best idea after all.

For years, Dean wouldn't come anywhere near the "big boy" rollercoasters, as I liked to call them. His bravery was reserved for what used to be called "The Space Needle", a slowly rotating cabin that inched its way up a tower that resembled a needle. It gave you a 360-degree view of the Charlotte area, all from the comforts of an air-conditioned cabin. After reaching the top, it brought you slowly and safely back to the ground.

Getting Dean to stand beneath a structure that actually *drops* you from that height and expecting him to actually get *on* it was unrealistic at best.

But let's back up a few years. Everyone knows that you don't start at "The Intimidator." You start somewhere much simpler.

Animation Station.
Boo Boo's Balloon Race.
Taxi Jam.

And finally, the rite of passage of all kid-themed roller-coasters:

Scooby Doo's Ghoster Coaster.

Painted purple, blue, and gold, this wooden coaster evoked images of the traditional train-car style of rides, just scaled down to a much smaller audience. Its first hill only went up a couple dozen feet from the platform, and it never got close to the break-neck speeds of the giants on the opposite end of the park. But for Dean, this was a big deal.

A really big deal.

I was nine years old at the time; Dean was almost fourteen. Our parents allowed us to walk up to the ride by ourselves while they positioned themselves on a bench beneath one of the first turns. Dean kept looking back over his shoulder to see where they would be, as if to plan his emergency escape route.

While waiting in line, Dean got quiet. This was bad news.

When Dean was looking forward to something, he would not stop talking. He spoke quickly and unhindered. He asked questions, answered those questions himself, and kept on talking. Excitement was never something Dean could hide.

If he was scared, however, he went silent. And whenever Dean's mouth stopped moving, the rest of his body would soon follow suit.

Remember the full-body paralysis I told you about? As we got to the front of the queue, waiting only for the next car to enter the station, that fear took hold.

"Dean, you okay?" I asked.

"I can't do this, Jon."

"Yes you can, Dean."

"No, Jon, I scared!"

"It's going to be okay, Dean. I promise."

"I do not know, Jon..."

Dean shook his head back-and-forth, showing his disbelief that his little brother was about to put him through this.

Tsssss... The hydraulics hissed as the next car came into the station. The lap-bars clicked and raised up as laughing children scampered off of the ride.

The gates to the queues opened, ushering us onto the awaiting ride. I stepped through first.

"Dean, are you coming?"

I turned to find Dean grasping both sides of the rails

outlining our queue. Frozen in fear, Dean aggressively shook his head.

One of the teenagers working the ride walked over to offer to help. I motioned him away. "I got it, he'll be okay," I said.

I walked back to Dean and put a hand on his shoulder and leaned in really close. His head was hung low, eyes locked on his feet, which might as well have been in cement blocks.

"Dean, look at me buddy."

He looked up. I could see the fear in his eyes. But beyond that, even at our young ages, I could see something else: Trust.

Dean always trusted what I had to say. Even if I as four-and-a-half years younger than him, whatever I said was his golden rule. He loved and trusted me with everything he had. I've always understood that this trust carried a great responsibility; one I couldn't take lightly.

"Dean," I whispered, knowing fully that whatever I said next would either embolden him to face his fears or send us both back to the bench where my parents awaited, "You just have to be brave enough to put the seatbelt on. You're brave. You can do this."

With that, Dean nodded and moved cautiously towards the car. I helped him into his seat, one slow step at a time, and followed him in.

Neither of us were ever small for our age, so we were squished into that train car like a subway during rush hour. I could barely lift my arms high enough to pull the lap-bar down.

It clicked once. I pushed further.

"Woah, woah, woah, Jon! Enough!"

Dean's bravery didn't require a second click.

The train lurched forward and we started up the first hill. I looked over at Dean. He held the lap-bar with both hands, his grip so tight his knuckles turned white. He immediately began pleading his case.

"Jon, I do not like this! I do not like this!"

"It's okay, Dean. It's okay. You're brave."

My efforts to console Dean clearly weren't enough.

As we reached the top of the hill, I offered one last reassurance.

"Dean, we're going to be okay."

Click. Drop.

"NO! WE'RE! NOOOOTTTTT!!!"

Dean screamed as we plummeted down the first hill. As we took a sharp left, the coaster shook us into each other, Dean's elbows dug into my ribs. Then, Dean's screams of fear turned into a half-scream, half-laugh.

"AHH-HA-HA-HAAA!!"

I began to belly-laugh at the sound of it. I held my arms above my head as the car whipped around the corners and over the crests of the small wooden hills. We rounded the final corner and the train threw us forward as it came to an abrupt stop. Laughter and sighs and high-fives broke out throughout the car. I looked at my brother.

"I love it! Let's do it again!" Dean exclaimed.

Just like that, Dean was brave enough to ride roller-coasters.

Over the next couple of years, Dean would gradually progress from the children's section of the park to the "big boy" rides. The Scooby Doo Ghoster Coaster gave way to its bigger, faster cousin, "Thunder Road." After conquering Thunder Road, Dean worked up the courage to tackle the Wayne's World staple, "The Hurler." I always thought that was the roughest ride in the park, my ribs always sore from being tossed around in the corners.

Perhaps Dean's crowning achievement in bravery was "Top Gun," which would be his very first upside-down roller coaster. In this ride, you sat in a seat fashioned after an airplane's cockpit and buckled yourself in using an over-the-shoulder harness. Your feet dangled beneath you to give the sensation of flying through the air.

Dean, ever the Tom Cruise fan, was the most excited to

conquer this ride. The first time he rode it, I watched him melt down in similar fashion to the Scooby Doo ride years prior. But I reminded him again, "Just be brave enough to put your seatbelt on."

I don't know if it was his trust in me or just the Kenny Loggins soundtrack playing overhead, but Dean stepped onto the platform and pulled down his shoulder harness as if he had done it a hundred times.

He looked at me, smiled, and said triumphantly, "I love you, Jon!" He gave me an emphatic fist bump.

After Top Gun, Dean led me onward to Vortex, Carolina Cyclone, and (many times over) the ice cream stand. By the time we found ourselves approaching the sign donning Dale Earnhardt's classic moniker, "The Intimidator," bravery was an old hat for Dean.

We both knew that Dean could do it, and I knew that he would reward me with his scream-laugh as we dropped down the first hill. It's worth it every time.

To this day, I've only ever purchased one photo print from the booth waiting at the end of a roller-coaster. Its green cardboard frame is giving way to the wear-and-tear of over twenty years of age now. But the artwork on the back of the frame is as unforgettable as the wide-eyed child death-gripping the lap-bar in the black-and-white photo: Scooby Doo's Ghoster Coaster.

I like to look at the photo at least once a month. It makes me laugh remembering the ridiculousness of it all; Dean's exaggerated expression makes this seem much more dramatic than a children's ride.

But more than that, it reminds me how brave Dean was. He never lost his fear of heights—he would routinely freeze and hold onto the stair rail of the upper levels of any sporting arena. But with a little encouragement, he would press on, reach the top of the stairs, buckle the seatbelt, or ride the ride.

And without fail, after he faced his fears and proved to himself that he could do it, Dean would flash his trademark grin and give a celebratory high-five, fist bump, or hug.

Dean taught me that it's okay to have fears. Everyone has them. But if you lean on the people who love you, you can dig down deep and prove to yourself that you are strong, brave, and capable. Even if you're on a rollercoaster.

7

NO MORE POOL PARTIES

Every year, Dean's attention focused on one of a few upcoming major events.

For example, when it came to his favorite sports teams, he knew the exact date of the first game of the season, that league's all-star game, and the first-year player draft.

Of course, there was also the Christmas season. To this day, I'm not entirely sure whether or not Dean still believed in Santa Claus, or if he just loved the tradition of Santa too much to say otherwise.

Either way, our family's entire goal each Christmas was to make it magical for Dean. He always wanted to help arrange the ornaments on the tree, being sure to put his favorite ornaments on the branches closest to where he would be sitting to open gifts on Christmas morning. We would bake cookies and pour a small glass of milk while Dean wrote a note to Santa Claus on Christmas Eve.

Each year, Dean would thank Santa and ask a new set of questions that he was curious about, like, "How do your reindeer fly?" Or, "How do you have time to visit every house?"

Each year, Dean would wait at the end of the hallway, refusing to go into the living room to see the Christmas tree until Bekah and I got there to join him. He would round the corner and gasp at the site of the gifts on the tree.

"Ah, cool!" Dean would shout, then shuffle to his place next to the tree. The next few hours would include Dean handing out the gifts to each person, celebrating each gift as we opened them. He would hand his wrapping paper to his dog, Molly, and laugh uproariously as she ripped it apart and frolicked in the pile she just made.

Then, the day after Christmas, he would inevitably ask, "How many days 'til next Christmas?"

In between Christmases, Dean also loved celebrating birthdays. Each Christmas, Dean received a new wall calendar upon which he could mark the dates to help him remember the birthdate of each person in the family. Then, without fail, as soon as his birthday became the next one up, he would start counting down the days.

"Jon, how long 'til my birthday?"

"Two months, Dean. It's getting close!"

"How many days that is?"

"About sixty, Dean."

"In sixty days, I be (insert age here) years old!"

"That's right, Dean. You're going to be an old man!" I would tease him.

But just as much as Christmas, birthdays, and the new sports seasons, Dean anticipated to his Special Olympics events with just as much passion.

Camp SOAR (Special Olympics Athletic Retreat) is week-long event gave both children and adults with intellectual and developmental disabilities the chance to participate in a day-camp filled with fun games, sports competitions, and even a dance. It was everything Dean loved—friends, sports, and dancing—in just one week.

Every June, Dean would "practice getting up early" to prepare for camp. Naturally, Dean would go to bed wearing the Camp SOAR t-shirt from the previous year and set his alarm clock to wake him up at seven o'clock every day for at least two weeks leading up to camp. You can't fault the man for wanting to be prepared!

After Camp SOAR would come Challenger Flag Football, and after that would come Dean's longest-running sport: Basketball.

Growing up in Charlotte, NC, in the glory days of the Charlotte Hornets, Dean and I would spend hours every day shooting on our backyard basketball goal. He would pretend to be Muggsy Bogues—after all, Dean and

Muggsy were the same height—and I would pretend to be Alonzo Mourning or Larry Johnson.

Which of us played the role of Hornets' sharpshooter Dell Curry? That would be Dean.

One look at Dean's smooth left-handed jump shot would tell you who the best shooter was in the family. We eventually had to switch from a nylon basketball net to a metal chain because Dean's shot would often swish into the net so crisply that it would rip the net in half.

Over the years, Dean's Special Olympics basketball teams accomplished a lot. They won gold medals seemingly every year. One year, their three-on-three team was so good that the local news filmed them at practice ahead of the Special Olympics State Games.

Many of Dean's teammates would graduate to the full-court, five-on-five league, while Dean stayed in three-on-three. The slower, half-court setup was more conducive to his ability (his lack of athleticism was more of an Adcock thing than a Down syndrome thing). The last few years of Dean's life, his teams weren't as successful, but Dean became an incredible passer. He seemed to get as much, if not more, satisfaction out of setting his teammates up to score with perfectly-placed passes as he did out of taking the shot himself.

That alone says a lot about Dean's selflessness—he knew how to celebrate others even better than he could celebrate himself. And Dean was good at celebrating himself.

Though flag football and basketball were Dean's favorites, he participated in a variety of other Special Olympics activities. He bowled for a while. When he was younger, he tried soccer, but that venture only lasted about a week.

Softball was perhaps the sport that Dean played the longest while not caring all that much about it.

Though Dean wasn't bad at softball, I always assumed that he only played it because I played baseball and this was the next-best thing.

As kids, we played baseball in the backyard with wiffle balls and plastic bats. Continuing with the approach we had for backyard basketball, we imitated our favorite professional baseball stars, all the way down to their swing. I loved the open stance and slow, menacing sway of Andres Galarraga, while Dean loved the high elbows and confident bat wiggle of Ken Griffey, Jr. Not to mention that Dean made sure to turn his hat around backwards whenever pretending to be the Mariners' legendary slugger. He was an earring away from true authenticity.

I believe that the hours we spent emulating the stars prepared Dean for softball, the same way mimicking Usher's slide steps prepared Dean to dance onstage at Night to Shine.

Dean's only problem with softball was that he didn't necessarily want to be good at softball. He just wanted to look good while he was playing.

That's why, when Dean stepped to the plate, he tapped the end of the bat on home plate twice. He flexed his arm ever-so-slightly as he did it too, causing the Nike emblem on his armband to rotate towards the pitcher's mound. Dean winked at the pitcher just before lifting his bat on his shoulder. (Confession... He never actually did that, but it would've been really cool if he did.)

Dean did, however, have the most beautiful, looping swing that evoked memories of Griffey himself.

But again, Dean was only there to look good. His swing, though picture-perfect, was so slow and deliberate that if he actually did hit the ball, it wasn't going very far. That didn't seem to bother Dean, as he would jog gently down the first-base line and give a smooth but convincing hand clap to make it look like he was frustrated with being thrown out.

Then, after returning to the bench, Dean was more than happy with sitting in the shade and spitting sunflower seeds.

Dean didn't have the same obsession with softball that he did with football or basketball, but he loved spending time with his friends and teammates nonetheless. That's why, whenever our family moved into a house with a big backyard and a swimming pool, Dean lobbied hard for us to turn the end-of-year banquet into a pool party at our house.

It would turn out to be the worst idea we ever had, albeit one of the most memorable.

Leading up to the 2005 Eagles Softball Pool-stravaganza (unofficially titled), we did our due diligence in preparing for a fun, but safe experience. The pool had a diving board and a maximum depth of over eight feet, and we were inviting over a group of teenagers with varying levels of physical limitations. Some of them could swim; others were anxious to even dip their toes into the shallow end of the pool.

We decided to buy and install a safety rope separating the shallow end from the deep end of the pool and assigned one of the parents, who was a lifeguard and swim coach, to keep watch over the pool while everyone was there. To help her out, we called each family listed on the team roster to see who could or couldn't swim. Confident we knew who to allow into the deep end and who needed to avoid it, we turned our attention towards buying hot dogs, filling the drink cooler with ice, and cutting watermelon for everyone to enjoy.

The only thing we didn't account for was that some of these kids were still in the "creatively mischievous" stage that Dean had finally grown out of.

Enter Jeffery.

Jeffery and Dean had been friends since they were in pre-school, and they rivaled each other in the race to see who had the most charisma and swagger. Jeffery is one of my favorite people in the entire world—he can make anyone laugh with his quick wit, and he was never afraid to talk trash when it came to competition.

Once, when I was volunteering as an assistant softball

coach for the Eagles, I decided to sit on the drink cooler while I tossed softballs for the players to hit into a net.

"What you sitting on that cooler for?" Jeffery asked.

"It helps me get lower to toss to you," I answered.

"Well lemme get something out of there first. What you got in there?"

"Just Gatorade and water. We'll get some after this drill."

"What you mean? What you talking about?"

"We just started, Jeffery. I'll make sure you stay hydrated. Let's just finish this drill first."

Jeffery shook his head. "Nah, man. You don't have none of that good stuff in there? None of that ack-o-hol?"

Jeffery's teammates erupted in laughter.

"C'mon, man!" I snapped back. "Alcohol? Ain't nobody having alcohol at practice!"

"I'm just asking, man! Just asking!" Jeffery threw his hands up and got back in line to hit into the net. Practice resumed.

Jeffery may have been joking around with me about the contents of my drink cooler, but on the day of the pool party, he was all business. A few hours before everyone was set to arrive, he called our house to tell us that he wouldn't be coming that day.

"Guys, I can't come to the party," Jeffery confessed.

"Why not, Jeffery? What's up?"

"I... I... I can't swim." Jeffery's voice dropped, embarrassed.

"Don't worry about that, Jeffery!" I told him. "Dean can't swim either. Neither can Dominique or half the other people on this team. Everybody's going to be hanging out in the shallow end, where all you have to do is stand up. You can do that!"

"Are you sure?" Jeffery asked, his spirits lifting.

"Absolutely, man. Your teammates would want you here! Come hang out!"

"Alright, I'll be there!" Jeffery exclaimed just before turning away from the phone to tell his mother that he wanted to go to the party after all.

We were all excited that Jeffery decided to come to the party. When he arrived, my parents made sure to show him where the shallow end was and Jeffery's mother reminded him not to jump off the diving board. Jeffery looked petrified at just the sight of the diving board, even though it only hovered about a foot above the water.

Jeffery's mom left, Jeffery joined his friends and teammates sitting around the pool, and all was well. I decided to go inside to refill the ice and bottled water in the drink cooler.

As I looked out the kitchen window, I saw an all-too-familiar site.

Jeffery was strutting around the perimeter of the pool, with a huge grin on his face. He was surely talking smack to someone; I assumed he was telling someone that he was a faster swimmer than them, even though Jeffery knew good-and-well he couldn't swim at all. It didn't matter though; it was all bravado. I smiled. I loved Jeffery's energy.

Then I saw Jefferey eye the diving board.

Uh-oh.

Then I saw Jeffery step onto the diving board.

"Wait. Jeffery can't swim. Jeffery knows he can't swim."

I saw a parent walk in Jeffery's direction, likely telling him to get off the diving board.

Then, just like that, Jeffery leapt off the diving board.

"Jeffery!" I dropped everything and sprinted outside.

Jeffery's body buoyed up out of the water and he had a big grin on his face, as if he just proved the world wrong about his ability.

Then he must've realized the error of his ways, because his eyes turned from pride to pure terror and he immediately sank beneath the surface.

The team panicked. Well, most of them did.

As our designated lifeguard dove in after Jeffery, his teammates either froze in fear or cried out his name, hoping that he was okay.

Again, most of them.

Dominique, who had Down syndrome, saw it as the perfect opportunity to do a cannonball off of the diving board.

He stutter-stepped into a big leap, bending his knees and launching himself off the end of the diving board and into the air. He wrapped his arms around his knees, twisting his body into the shape of a cannonball. The water thumped and splashed upwards, just a couple feet from where the lifeguard was now pulling Jeffery out of the pool.

That's when we remembered.

Dominique couldn't swim either.

Another parent dove in and pulled Dominique out of the water while Jeffery flailed his arms, now screaming, "Dominique! Dominique!"

Within seconds, both of them were completely fine. They were safely rescued from the pool just as quickly as they jumped in. But also just as quickly, the pool party was over.

"Alright, everybody out!" I don't remember who yelled it, but everyone listened.

"If we're not going to follow the rules, no one is going to swim!"

That didn't seem to bother this Eagles softball team, as they shortly resumed splashing in the pool—in the shallow end this time—and snacking on watermelon and hot dogs.

Dominique was entirely unfazed by the whole incident, as he proceeded to load the entire bowl of chili onto two hot dogs, all while his teammates waited in line behind him.

Jeffery was laughing about everything almost immediately, holding a washable marker to his lips like it was a cigar as he spoke confidently about how he knew what he was doing the whole time.

Dean spent most of his time dancing with Robin, twirling her around and two-stepping to the 1960's beach music playing on the battery-powered boombox.

At the end of the day, it was a fantastic end-of-season pool party.

It just happened to also be the last one we would ever host.

Watching my brother participate in the Special Olympics taught me a lot of valuable life lessons. It taught me the value of teamwork long before I ever played sports myself. It taught me how to compete hard, but have fun doing it.

And most importantly, it taught me how to be brave.

Not jump-in-the-pool-when-you-can't-swim brave. That's more foolish than anything.

But it taught that whenever life presents an obstacle or limitation, be it something you're born with or something that just happened to you in the moment, the bravest thing you can do is face it head-on. Lean on your teammates and, with their support, conquer that obstacle.

Special Olympics has an oath that they ask all athletes to recite at any of their opening ceremonies. It says this:

"Let me win. But if I cannot win, let me be brave in the attempt."

Sometimes, you'll jump off that diving board, bounce right back up to the surface, and keep on swimming. Other times, life will feel more like you were pushed off of a diving board and into the deep end when you know you can't swim.

Either way, your response is up to you. Be brave simply because you can. Life's more rewarding when you choose to be brave.

8

"ON THE THIRD DAY…"

Dean always knew how to ask questions. Lots of questions.

One of his favorite things to ask about was people's ages:

"Jon, how old was I when Panthers started playing?"

"Dean, you were eleven years old."

"Jon, how old you were when Panthers started playing?"

"I was six."

"Hm."

He always ended his conversations with this inquisitive-sounding grunt that only told me that more questions were coming.

"Jon, how old Michael Jackson was when he did Thriller?"

"Dean, I have no idea."

"Hm."

It didn't matter the subject; the questions were endless. But the questions that always kept me on my toes were the ones pertaining to God, Jesus, and the Bible.

Dean and I weren't raised in church, but we spent our summers with our hardcore-Southern-Baptist grandmother. She made sure we were at every Vacation Bible School she could find and she did everything she could to make sure we had an opportunity to know who Jesus was.

In the Bible, Jesus talked about coming to him with a childlike faith (Matthew 18); a level of trust that mirrored the way a child lovingly looks to and depends on his or her parents for every single thing in life. It's not built on blind ignorance, but rather a loving trust and understanding that there is someone much bigger and more powerful than me that is going to make sure everything is okay.

That's how Dean came to faith in Jesus, and that's how he remained throughout his life.

Dean and I gave our lives to Christ at one of those Vacation Bible Schools. That is, we prayed the prayer and truly believed that Jesus died and was resurrected from the grave after three days so that we could be forgiven of our sin.

We briefly went to a church around the time I was entering high school, all because I was invited to play on their baseball team that Spring. Dean and I both were baptized there, a ceremonial act meant to publicly profess our faith in Jesus.

At that church, one of the pastors gave Dean a "Teen Adventure Bible," a full Bible in large enough print for him to read and in a translation he could understand (Translation: No "thee's" and "thou's").

Dean didn't just try to read that Bible; he tried to understand as much as he could. He would constantly ask me questions about what he read, not shying away from some hard topics.

"Jon, why David kill Bathsheba's husband?"

Or, "Jon, how old was Peter?"

And my favorite line of questioning:

"Jon, who was David's dad?"

"That was Jesse, Dean."

"Hm. How 'bout Jesse's dad?"

"I'd have to check on that one, Dean.""

"You not know that, Jon?"

"Nah, Dean. Not off the top of my head."

"Hm."

He kept me on my toes.

But despite, or even because of, his inquisitive nature, Dean had a pure sense of who God is and how He loves each and every one of us.

Dean would routinely ask to say the blessing before any family meals, which would force us to remind him, "Dean, say a prayer this time, not a sermon."

He would shake his head in frustration before launching into a solid two-to-three-minute prayer complete with phrases like, "God, we are all your people," and, "You saved all of us from our sins," and would rarely ever get around to anything pertaining to the food in front of us.

But the staple in all of his prayers was an emphasis on God loving all people. He even had a laminated placemat for his spot at the dinner table that read, in his child-like handwriting, "God's forgiveness is for all who believe in Him."

Dean didn't waste time worrying about who qualified for God's love and acceptance. He didn't care about someone's past mistakes, social standing, or sexuality. None of the stuff that seems to bother all the church-goers on the news seemed to matter to Dean, which is why I think his faith may have been exactly what God wanted.

To Dean, the essence of Christianity could be broken down into these three phrases:

1. God loves all of us, no matter what.
2. Jesus accepts anyone, so we should too.
3. We're supposed to love people, especially if they're different from us.

In fact, Dean would get sincerely upset any time he saw people spewing hate on the news in the name of Christianity.

"Jon, why these people hate other people?" he would ask me. "Hate is wrong."

Dean's heart, in my opinion, was as pure as anyone I've ever met. Sure, he had his mischievous tendencies as a kid, but as he got older, he could not operate without a sense of sincerity and kindness. If he did something wrong, like talking back to my mom or dad, he would almost immediately feel remorseful and go give them a hug and say, "I sorry. I love you."

Once, when Dean was at Ms. Suzanne's small group for young adults with disabilities, she led an activity where she asked each of the dozen or so guests, "Tell me something you did this week that you felt bad about."

The goal was to identify something they could apologize and ask forgiveness for, using it as an illustration to show them how God will always forgive them too.

Dean made it a little more difficult when he couldn't think of anything.

Suzanne asked Dean, "Are you sure Dean? You didn't have one bad day this week?"

"No, Ms. Suzanne. I never have a bad day," he replied.

He was right. Dean lived every day with love and trust and sincere joy. It's hard to be bothered or to act out when you live that way.

Why am I telling you all of this?

It's not because I think Dean is perfect, although he is as close as anyone I'll ever know. It's more to set the stage for how Dean's sincere and childlike-approach to the spiritual world would affect my life forever.

Dean and I were both born with the same genetic heart condition, hypertrophic cardiomyopathy. Basically, our hearts are enlarged, which can affect a number of things, but primarily blood flow in and out of the heart and how well the heart stays in rhythm.

Because of this, we both have ICDs (implantable cardioverter defibrillators) implanted in our chests, which are meant to shock and restart our hearts in the event of a life-threatening arrhythmia.

Thankfully, Dean never had to experience any shocks from his defibrillator. I, on the other hand, have depended on my device to save my life a number of times.

When a defibrillator shocks a heart, it will ideally need

just one shock to restart the heart and restore its normal rhythm. It's considered sudden cardiac arrest, so the sooner you restore your heartbeat, the better your chances are of survival. On the other hand, the longer you go without oxygen, the more likely you are to have permanent and severe brain and organ damage.

In late-March 2016, on an otherwise normal Friday evening, my defibrillator failed.

I returned to the house from walking our pug, and within thirty seconds, I felt the sensation of my heartbeat stopping. I had enough time to sit down and tell my wife, "I'm about to get shocked."

She had never seen it happen before, so she expected what I told her to expect, which was, "If it ever happens, just give me a second. I'll come back and be okay."

That didn't happen.

A few seconds turned into a minute, and a minute into two, and I still had no pulse.

Panicked, my wife called 911 while her sister, who had just arrived at our house for a weekend visit, started chest compressions.

Even after paramedics arrived, neither my device nor the chest compressions could restart my heart. According to my wife Bekah, I was without a pulse for at least forty-five minutes and at most an hour and a half.

After rushing me to the hospital and sweeping my wife

and family into a waiting room, doctors eventually restarted my heart. After seventeen shocks from a defibrillator and many minutes of CPR, I was alive again. But in an attempt to slow any organ damage caused by such a prolonged period of time without oxygen, they entered me into a "Code Cool" protocol, where doctors essentially chilled my body and induced a hypothermic coma for up to three days.

By that point, my entire family and many of our friends were in the hospital, waiting, praying, and believing together that I would survive.

My parents and Dean visited my room before leaving for the night. My parents were afraid that Dean would be overwhelmed by the number of IVs and tubes attached to my body. But he was remarkably cool, calm, and collected.

As they were walking out of my room to return home for the night, Dean stopped in the doorway and turned to look at Bekah and me.

Without a hesitation in his voice, he said, "On the third day, he rose."

He turned and walked out of the room.

That's when it hit everyone:

It was Good Friday. This was the day Jesus died, and three days prior to the moment he was resurrected from the grave.

Dean's matter-of-fact statement flipped a switch in the room. No longer were despair and distress in charge; faith took over.

From that Friday night until Sunday morning, we were showered with endless messages of prayer and encouragement from our friends and church family, with each one of them centered around this "third-day" mentality. Several doctors informed my wife that she needed to draft a will for my estate, as the likelihood of my survival was very low, and even if I made it through, I went without oxygen for so long that I may not have any brain function.

Perhaps you've discovered the spoiler alert by picking up this book and seeing my name on the front cover:

I made it.

Doctors began to wake me up from my sedation on Easter Sunday. One by one, they removed my ventilator and sedation medications and began to warm my body back to a normal temperature.

By the following day, I was back.

Dean was elated to see his brother awake and speaking again. Aside from a drug-induced short-term memory loss that lasted only a few days, there were no lingering effects of my cardiac arrest. I was able to chat college basketball with Dean and listen to him speculating who the Carolina Panthers would draft in April.

Every couple of days from that moment until Dean

passed away, he and I would talk about how he said, "On the third day..." We would shake our heads at how crazy those few days were. I'd give him a big hug and thank him for believing that I would be okay, and for checking on my wife Bekah during that time.

"Of course, Jon. I love my sister-in-law Bekah. I love you too, Jon."

Later, I had "ON THE THIRD DAY" tattooed on my right forearm, which caused Dean to immediately want a matching tattoo. I offered several times to take him to the tattoo shop, but as soon as he remembered that needles were involved, he backed off.

To me, the most permanent reminder of my own miracle isn't the ink beneath my skin; it's how my Down syndrome brother sparked an entire community of family, friends, and even strangers to believe for the impossible. I believe it helped to save my life.

This book is not meant to be an exposé on Dean's faith and why you should convert to Christianity. Not at all. But it would be remiss to not mention Dean's pure, inquisitive, and child-like faith. He wasn't afraid to believe the impossible could happen, especially if it affected someone he loved. He never wavered in his belief that I would be okay, and smiled afterwards as if he knew the outcome all along.

I want that for myself. Hundreds of people drafted off of Dean's faith that weekend. Honestly, I still am, too.

Even if I never catch up to the sincerity of Dean's faith,

I've at least learned this from him:

Love everyone. But bring closest to you the kind of people who will not back down from even the most impossible circumstances, simply because they love you. Stand arm-in-arm with those people, for they will be the ones holding you up when you can't stand for yourself.

And never, ever give up. Because God hasn't given up on you.

9

COACH DEAN

Growing up in the 1990s, Dean and I were obsessed with sports. More specifically, we were obsessed with our local sports team in Charlotte, the Carolina Panthers and Charlotte Hornets.

That's why, when the Carolina Panthers partnered with Mecklenburg County Parks & Recreation to form a flag football league for youth and young adults with disabilities, Dean was all-in from the start.

The concept was simple: Create an opportunity to compete for kids who would otherwise never get the chance to participate in the sport of football.

Growing up, Dean was involved in numerous sports through Special Olympics, including basketball, softball, bowling, tennis, and track and field. And if you know the Adcock family athletic gene pool, you know that track and field is a sport we should never, ever participate in.

But Dean did it all. And he loved every bit of it.

Yet, for fairly obvious safety reasons, football had yet to take off in the Special Olympics world in North and South Carolina. For Dean and me, we got our football fix from tossing the ball around in the backyard and occasionally going one-on-one to try to tackle each other.

Dean always dreamed of being a quarterback. It makes sense, given his propensity for the spotlight, for him to want to take charge as the leader of a team and assume the position that is most likely to garner all notoriety. But Dean had a beautiful, left-handed spiral that he could throw with remarkable accuracy. His throws may not have had the velocity of Cam Newton, but Dean was able to put the ball where it was supposed to go, which made him a perfect quarterback.

When the Panthers' sponsorship of Challenger Flag Football came around in the early 2000's, and later their funding of Special Olympics Flag Football in the Carolinas, Dean gained a stage on which to display some of his greatest gifts.

In the special needs community, there is a vast spectrum of intellectual and social ability. Though Dean wasn't as intellectually advanced as some of his peers, his social skills were off the charts. Most of his friends looked to Dean as their thermostat; he set the social temperature in every room he stepped into. When something needed to happen, if Dean knew what to do, the entire group would know exactly what to do. He included everyone. And as much he loved the limelight, he loved celebrating other people just as much.

All of this translated perfectly to the flag football field: Dean called the plays, made sure everyone got the ball, and went over-the-top in celebrating each play. There was even a season where Dean coordinated his team's touchdown celebrations to imitate Steve Smith, their favorite Panthers' player.

For at least ten Saturday's between September and November, Challenger Flag Football gave Dean the chance to be the quarterback of his dreams. He would drop beautiful passes over the secondary and into his receiver's waiting hands. He'd sprint down the sideline to meet his teammates in the end zone for a special touchdown dance—perhaps my favorite of which was Dean placing the ball gently on the ground, tilting up one end, and wiping the bottom of it as if it was a baby receiving a diaper change.

Playing flag football kept Dean active, helped him make new friends, and grew his confidence, which was never lacking in the first place.

One season, they held their final games on the Carolina Panthers' practice field, immediately following an official team practice.

Dean, never shy, stopped Jake Delhomme, the Panthers' starting quarterback at the time, as he left the field.

"Hey Jake! Guess what? I'm a quarterback too."

Jake's face lit up as he high-fived Dean. He started to

chat with Dean before a team staffer pulled Jake away for an on-camera interview. But the moment was already made for Dean. He beamed from ear-to-ear. Then he proceeded to go out on to the big field and make some of the best throws of his entire life.

The Challenger Flag Football League was rightfully Dean's most-anticipated activity of the year.

The only downside of the program was the age limit: Players were only allowed to play until they were 25 years old. For Dean, that meant that 2009 would be his last season as a player in the Challenger Flag Football League.

But the first time we broke the news to Dean, we told him, "You know this is your last season as a player, right?"

Without hesitation, Dean replied back, "When I retire, I want to be a coach."

In his mind, it was as simple as deciding whether or not to brush your teeth in the morning. He was retiring this season—not aging out—and he was going to coach next year.

Just like that.

His final season came and went, and Dean retired. Several of his friends and original participants in the Challenger Flag Football league aged-out of the program as well.

But the following summer, when Dean would normally start watching Panthers' highlights and talking about the plays he wanted to run that Fall, he was reminding us that this would be his first year coaching. So off we went to the Marion-Diehl Center to pick up Dean's volunteer registration and background-check forms.

(If we were going to do this thing, we were going to do it the right way.)

Good news: Dean's background check cleared!

And that September, Dean stepped onto that artificial turf with an ever-greater sense of excitement. If playing flag football helped him realize his dreams, coaching helped him fulfill his purpose.

As a Challenger Flag Football League Coach, Dean was an encourager. He was a teacher. He was a leader. Each of the players on the field looked to Dean for direction on where to line up, what route to run, where to throw the ball, and at the end of the play, for a high-five or a hug telling them, "Good job!"

There are a few players in the league who utilize powered wheelchairs. They often need extra assistance, so a "buddy" is typically assigned to each of them. Their buddy's job is to make sure they're lined up and moving in the right direction, catch any passes thrown their direction, and quickly hand them the football so that they can motor down the field.

Dean was always mindful of how each of these wheelchair-using athletes were doing. Dean made sure to get the ball to each of them a handful of times per game, sometimes drawing up a trick play that would leave them wide-open in the end zone for a touchdown. Dean always made a point of making them feel included.

Dean walked—actually, "strutted" might be more accurate—away from the field each week with a huge smile on his face. He would talk all the way to the car about how cool it was to see his friend Stuart score, or how great of a catch Christian made.

Then he'd get in the car and be asleep and snoring before we left the parking lot.

Dean gave everything he had to those few hours on Saturday mornings. Even though he was aged-out of the program as a player, he would return every year for eight seasons to coach on the Challenger Flag Football League sidelines.

His selfless commitment to the league set an example for the entire community. Dean's coaching inspired a few other special-needs athletes to volunteer in various capacities after they aged out of the program. Panthers' Head Coach Ron Rivera heard about Dean and sent him an autographed coaches' visor and polo, which became Dean's coaching uniform for each and every game. Even Tom Sorensen, a longtime columnist for The Charlotte Observer, heard of Dean and dedicated an entire column to Dean's story.

When Dean saw his picture on the front page of the Sports section, with the bolded headline, "Dean, a Team, and Dream," he smiled triumphantly.

"I famous again!"

Yes, Dean. Yes you were.

He may not have been an NFL head coach, pulling the strings on nationally-televised games, but he made a difference. His joy was contagious. He knew everyone's name. He could recall something that each player loved, just to spark a conversation that would make them to smile. He made sure no one was left out.

That sounds like a winning coach to me.

There are dozens of adult volunteers and staff who make the Challenger Flag Football League incredible each and every season. A handful have been involved since the start, and the league wouldn't be what it is without them. Neither would the young men and women participating in the league be who they are today without these faithful people's influence.

If you ever get the chance to volunteer or be a part of something like the Challenger Flag Football League, do it. You'll go into it thinking it's a great opportunity to help someone else, but you'll leave feeling like they were helping you.

Because right in the middle of it all, from the huddle to the sideline, there's someone like Dean:

The heart and soul of Challenger Flag Football.

10

THE SUPER BOWL
(AND OTHER COOL THINGS)

Dean's unmistakable swag and charisma earned him
favor with anyone he met. That favor led to him getting
to do a lot of things that most of us only dream of doing.
And as Dean's brother, I unashamedly rode his coattails
into some incredibly cool places.

Like the time Dean got to dribble one-on-one with
Charlotte Hornets' point guard Muggsy Bogues at a
Special Olympics clinic. Then, years later, through
connections with one of my best friends, Muggsy
himself surprised Dean on his birthday by having him
over at his house to play one-on-one and eat cupcakes.

Or maybe the time we got to go onto the field at Bank
of America Stadium before a Carolina Panthers'
preseason game. Dean got to run out of the tunnel; I got
to hang out on the sideline.

Or the time the Panthers brought a group of special-needs athletes (Dean included) to a regular season game against the Arizona Cardinals. We all got to be on the sideline during pre-game warm-ups, where all-time great Steve Smith took the time to speak to and take pictures with each member of our group, then gave each of them official NFL game balls.

And since we're talking about the Panthers, there was also the time Dean got to be a special guest at a Super Bowl Pep Rally breakfast at a swanky country club just days before the Panthers played in Super Bowl 50. While I sat at the table next to the team's owner, Dean got to go onstage with his "buddy" and Panthers' Community Relations Director, Riley Fields, to lead the entire room in an energetic hand-clap routine.

But nothing will ever compare to the phone call my family received from Riley Fields at the end of 2017:

"So we can't tell Dean, but the Panthers want to send Dean to Minneapolis for Super Bowl 52."

It was the most difficult secret I've ever had to keep in my entire life.

Unfortunately, the Panthers' playoff run ended a couple weeks later with a first-round loss to the New Orleans Saints. But even without our favorite team in the running to make the Super Bowl, Dean was lobbying for a Super Bowl party at our house.

"Jon, I want to get pizza. Jet's—the good stuff! And you

and Bekah make chips and salsa. How 'bout that? That a good idea?"

"Absolutely Dean. You get to call the shots this year. You make the menu."

"Cool, Jon! I think I want wings too. I think."

It took everything in me not to tell him, "Dean, where we're going, you're not going to be worried about wings."

Finally, on January 22, 2018, we got to watch Dean receive the surprise of a lifetime.

We told him that the Carolina Panthers were hosting a "Challenger Flag Football Coaches Summit" and that he was a special guest. There would be coaches from Charlotte and the surrounding areas ready to dissect plays and discuss ways to improve their coaching skills.

Dean was elated. The night before, he dug a zip-up binder and legal pad from one of his desk drawers. He was saving it for a special occasion (trust me, Dean was always ready for the next big and amazing thing to happen). He asked me to help him spell "Challenger" and "Summit" so he could appropriately title the top of the first page in the notebook. On the following pages, he drew up a few offensive plays, just like the X's and O's he had seen coaches draw on chalkboards in the locker room scenes of football movies and NFL Films specials.

On the way to the Panthers' stadium that morning, Dean

would not stop talking. Our entire family went—my mom, dad, my wife Bekah, and Dean all crammed into a Toyota RAV-4. He asked questions about who would be there, whether or not he would get to see Cam Newton, and if we thought Greg Olsen would win the "Walter Payton Man of the Year" award in a few weeks.

He had no idea that he would meet Greg face-to-face in just a few minutes.

Once we arrived, Riley walked us into the Team Meeting Room, a room resembling a lecture hall, but filled with plush, oversized, leather chairs. Only true sports fans will understand why I got goosebumps thinking about who may have sat in these seats before we got there. Dean alternated between grinning ear-to-ear and clicking his pen, ready to take notes.

On the screen was the Panthers' logo, along with the words "2018 Challenger Flag Football Coaches Summit." Unbeknownst to Dean, the room was filled with Panthers staff members, not flag football coaches.

Riley welcomed everyone to the summit and welcomed a special guest, Panthers' Pro Bowl tight end Greg Olsen.

Dean gasped and elbowed me in the ribs.

Greg walked into the room and apologized, letting everyone know that there would be no Coaches Summit. Dean was immediately concerned.

But then, Greg said, "Is Dean Adcock here?"

Dean looked at me wide-eyed, as if to say, "Me? Is he asking for me?"

Greg motioned for Dean to come up to the front of the room and said, "Dean, I hear you're the one with all the plays."

"Yes, I am," Dean said. He never lacked confidence.

For the next few moments, I could tell Dean was in awe. He looked up at one of his heroes, and for one of the only times in his life, was quiet.

"Well, Dean… Today we've got a special surprise for you. Are you ready?"

"Uh-huh!"

"We are sending you to Super Bowl 52, with a guest, tickets, hotel, airfare, on us. Just for being such a big Panthers fan and such an awesome dude."

Dean froze.

"Is this something you want to do, because we can give it to someone else," Greg asked.

"YEAH! I'm going!!" Dean yelled.

Greg apologized for the Panthers not being in the game, but Dean interrupted him.

"Next year, the Panthers can do it!"

Dean's nerves had worn off.

Then as they posed for pictures, Dean interrupted again.

"Greg, can I say something?"

"Sure, buddy, go ahead."

"My favorite team for college is University of Miami. The U!" Dean held both hands up, with his thumbs extended and touching each other, forming a big "U", made famous by the University of Miami football team—where Greg Olsen played.

Quick side note—Dean wasn't a University of Miami fan. He loved the ESPN 30 for 30 film on how their football teams changed college football culture. But as for his fandom, he only wanted to shout them out because he knew Greg Olsen would appreciate it.

I'm telling you… You just can't teach swag.

There they were: Dean, Greg Olsen, and mascot "Sir Purr", all three holding up "The U" for a photo-op.

"That's my brother," is all I could think.

That, and, "Well, somebody's got to take him to the Super Bowl. Might as well be me."

11

THE SUPER BOWL

PART (FIFTY-)TWO

Dean didn't even wait to get home before he started planning what he and I would do on our trip to Minnesota.

On the way out of the stadium, fresh off of being surprised by one of his favorite Carolina Panthers, Dean was bouncing up-and-down, talking about who was going to win and how excited he was to see Justin Timberlake at halftime ("I hope he plays 'Dirty Pop' from *NSYNC!").

Then he stopped on the sidewalk. Something hit him like a ton of bricks.

"What's wrong, Dean?" I stopped to check on him. My parents and my wife walked ahead, unaware that we had just stopped.

"Jon, we going to get in trouble in Minnesota?"

"What are you talking about? Dean, there's nothing to get in trouble for. We're going to the Super Bowl!"

"No, Jon. We going to the club while we're in Minnesota?"

I hit him with the giant foam Super Bowl ticket they gave us to commemorate the surprise.

"Boy! You JUST found out you're going to the Super Bowl and you're trying to go to the club?! We're NOT going to no clubs!"

"I just asking, Jon!" Dean threw his hands up and started walking again. "Just asking!"

I threw my arm around his shoulders and laughed. "It's going to be a brothers trip, alright?"

"Alright, Jon. Brothers trip!"

Two weeks later, I found myself in an airport, coaching Dean on how to handle the popping in his ears during takeoff. Never a stranger to anyone, Dean was quick to tell every airline attendant, "This my first time on an airplane!"

One attendant gave Dean a pin in the shape of airplane wings, which he proudly wore all day long. He couldn't believe that the pack of cookies and the cup of soda were free, or that he could watch a movie at his seat. He hardly watched the screen, however, as his window seat meant he could stare out the window in awe of the land below. I kept my screen on our flight tracker because every few minutes, he would point to something and ask, "Jon, where are we now?"

Once we landed, my job was simple: Protect Dean from the Minnesota cold.

One of the challenges people with Down syndrome face is with their immune systems. Dean was always more susceptible to respiratory illnesses, as he developed pneumonia dozens of times growing up. A simple cough could turn into a hospital stay if we weren't careful, so I knew not to take the sub-zero temperatures in Minneapolis lightly.

The day before the Super Bowl, I layered Dean with long-johns, long-sleeve hunting shirts, winter jackets, knit hats, and gloves. I circled the parking lots in our rental car until a parking spot opened up close to wherever we were going, just to minimize time outside in the cold.

Dean didn't seem to mind—I played Justin Timberlake on the car stereo (Dean's request was to only listen to the artist performing at halftime) and he sang the entire time.

That morning, we ventured out to downtown Minneapolis for the Super Bowl Experience, an open-to-the-public event with various exhibits, displays, and even live sports broadcasts. I decided we needed to try a local restaurant known for their blueberry pancakes, so I

drove our tiny rental car off the highway and into a
residential area.

I didn't realize that the residential area roads would be
packed tight with snow, something us North Carolina
boys didn't see very often. I drove slowly and carefully
on the all-white roads, being sure to stay in my lane and
away from other cars. Less than a mile from our
restaurant, I signaled to make our final turn of the trip, a
right-hand turn where we had the green turn arrow. I
slowed to about ten miles per hour and started the turn.

Suddenly, I felt my snow-driving fears coming true—the
rear wheels slid out from underneath me, I tried to steer
with skid, and now I'm in a full-blown 360-degree spin.
The snow crunched and I held my breath, fortunate to
complete the spin and keep going without hitting
anything.

Then it hit me—Dean is going to snitch on me. I could
already hear him, "Hey mom! We just ate breakfast. I
had pancakes. They were good. Jon wrecked the car."

I turned to Dean, ready to beg for his silence. He was
asleep. Aggressively asleep. His head was back, mouth
was open, and he was snoring. I forgot that Dean also
had the gift of being able to sleep through anything,
especially in the car.

We were safe. And more importantly, I was safe from
him getting me in trouble.

I looked over at the little pancake house on the side of
the road and assumed that if we couldn't make that slow

turn, we didn't stand a chance in the piles of snow in their parking lot. I made a U-turn and drove straight to the Super Bowl Experience.

After I parked the car (and woke Dean up), Dean was in the sports-equivalent of Disney World. He wanted to do everything. The Virtual Reality booth. The line to see the Lombardi Trophy. The Super Bowl Rings display. The set of "NFL Live". The Madden video game booth. We did it all.

Dean even jumped in line for two obstacle course activities. At one, he had to dodge a couple targets, scramble to his left, and throw a football into a waiting target. The other had him high step through an agility ladder, run through a set of hanging heavy bags, and dive onto a landing mat that represented the end zone. Dean did it all with his signature swagger—his left-handed throw glided effortlessly toward the target, and his end zone dive culminated in a celebration where he pretended to rip open his shirt, a la Superman, and then dab, a la Cam "Superman" Newton.

By the time we got dinner at the Mall of America, we were both exhausted. We tried to go to bed early at the hotel, but were both too excited to fall asleep. The next day, after all, was the Super Bowl.

The next morning, I woke up to a weather report of negative six degrees. It "felt like" negative thirteen. Side note—I've never understood the "felt like" temperature. If it feels like it's thirteen below zero, dang it, it's thirteen below zero.

I ventured out to get us breakfast from McDonalds—
I'm proud to say I didn't spin out the car this time—and
woke Dean up when I returned. Dean's first response
was to sit up, find his little flip-phone that he was
immensely proud of, and call my mom.

"Mom, I up! I awake! Guess what—Jon got McDonalds
for breakfast!"

He was always the most excited about the smallest
things.

After eating our breakfast and watching some of the pre-
game coverage on television, we suited in up in our
matching Greg Olsen jerseys (he did gift us the tickets; it
was the least we could do), and set out for the game.

Because the city was shut down within a mile of the
stadium, we took the light rail from the Mall of America
all the way to US Bank Stadium in the heart of
downtown Minneapolis. I helped Dean position himself
close to an exit door where he could easily hold onto a
handrail. We laughed as the train lurched forward and
both of us struggled to keep our balance.

"Look Jon!" Dean pointed out the window, smiling and
wide-eyed. "Snow!"

As the train whizzed down the tracks, Dean marveled at
the piles of snow covering the ground. I'm sure it was
commonplace for anyone who was local to the area. But
to us, this was special.

We were several hours early for the game, on purpose. I

wanted us to take in every second of this experience and not rush a thing. We met the other couple that the Carolina Panthers sent to the Super Bowl for free—a couple recognized for being "Fans of the Year" and the organizers of a fantastic summer camp for children with cancer, Camp Care. We bought overpriced stadium food, walked around the stadium, and took so many pictures. Dean and I were both in Heaven.

Then came time to go to our seats. We had no idea where our seats would be until we got there, and frankly, we didn't care. We were at the Super Bowl!

But as it turned out, our seats were in the very last row at the very top of the upper level.

Remember the fear of roller-coasters? As it also turned out, Dean was still extremely scared of heights.

And again, when I say, "Dean was extremely scared of heights," I don't mean, "Dean got nervous and had a hard time looking down when we were up high." I mean, "Dean panicked and completely shut down whenever he had to climb stairs to the top of a stadium."

Whenever I took him to Panthers games or Charlotte Hornets games, I would either splurge on lower-level seats, or buy seats at the very bottom of the upper level so he wouldn't have to climb any stairs. But in the event that we did have to climb a lot of stairs, I was the only person in the world who could coax him all the way to the top.

So that's what I did. One step at a time. It only took

somewhere around 108 "You got this" encouragements to get him to our seats. When we got there, I gave him a big hug and told him, "You did it Dean! Look how brave you are! And dude... We're at the Super Bowl!"

Still, Dean refused to look down at the field for a solid fifteen minutes. I gave him space, helped him take some deep breaths, and even resorted to recording a few selfie videos to send back home to Mom and Dad. But he still couldn't do it. He still couldn't look down. I would try to say, "Look at the scoreboard, Dean!" Or, "Look, Tom Brady is out there!"

Nothing.

Then, over the public address system, came the words, "Now performing at Super Bowl Live, Darius Rucker!"

Dean's head shot up. Darius welcomed the crowd and strummed his guitar to start the first song.

"Jon, look! It's Hootie!"

Dean jumped to his feet and started dancing like he was on stage with the band.

That's all it took. It wasn't the pep talks, the atta-boys, or any of his brother's help. Dean just needed Hootie.

The rest of the night, Dean was in his element. We didn't sit down for a second of the game. He was pulling for the Philadelphia Eagles because my wife Bekah is originally from Philadelphia. He was also quick to point out that he was also pulling for the New England

Patriots running back, Dion Lewis, simply because he went to high school with Bekah.

He danced to every song during every timeout. He yelled and cheered at every play throughout the game. He high-fived Eagles fans and complimented them on their Eagles jerseys. He blew kisses to the cheerleaders. I don't know what the people around us expected when they saw this young man with Down syndrome in a Carolina Panthers jersey, but Dean impressed them in typical Dean fashion.

A few of the more intoxicated fans would see our jerseys and ask us, "The Panthers? Greg Olsen?"

To which Dean would reply, "Yep! He my favorite player. I like your jersey too. Number 36, Brian Westbrook. He was a good running back."

"You know who Brian Westbrook is?" One guy asked.

"Yeah! My favorite Eagle though is Brian Dawkins. He played Clemson University."

"Wow, that's right!"

Of course he was right. Dean knew his football. And he knew how to win people over.

By halftime, Dean was the star of our section. Everyone turned and watched as he danced and sang every word to every song Justin Timberlake performed. When a drape fell from the ceiling and JT launched into "Purple Rain" by the hometown-legend Prince, Dean broke out the air guitar and threw his head back as if he was tossing around his own perfectly-permed curls.

For a night, Dean was the biggest star on the biggest stage in the entire world. As the Eagles went blow-for-blow with Tom Brady and the Patriots, with backup quarterback Nick Foles even catching a touchdown pass on the now-infamous "Philly Special" play, Super Bowl 52 became one of the best title games in NFL history. But it was Dean's moment in the spotlight, too.

I watched Dean as much as I watched the game that night. The joy in his eyes was as pure and as full as I'd ever seen it in my entire life. He gave me at least a dozen hugs throughout the game and told me, "I love you, Jon!"

After the game, we made our way down from the last row in the stadium to the very first, as the ushers allowed us to walk all the way down to the front row in the end zone to watch the post-game festivities. We sat down for one of the first times all night and stayed for about two hours after the game's final whistle.

The field and seats alike were covered in confetti. Several Eagles players made confetti angels on their backs in the middle of the end zone. Running back Jay Ajayi draped the English flag over his shoulder pads and hugged his mom over the railing. Super Bowl MVP Nick Foles gushed about his team's performance from the post-game press conference.

I looked around the stadium, and tears filled my eyes. I couldn't believe that we were here. The Super Bowl. The biggest football game in the world. Millions of people watch this on television every year, and we were here. In person. And not only that, our favorite team, the team we had grown up with, watching or listening to every game since their inception, thought enough of my brother Dean to send the two of us here for free.

I just couldn't comprehend why we were so lucky. How did Dean and I get to do something like this?

In that moment, something came from deep within my soul to impress one specific thought upon me.

"You're going to need this moment."

It floored me. I didn't know what to make of it, but I felt the need to look at Dean and etch this memory into my brain forever. I didn't know why or when, but I knew I needed it.

"Dean, I love you buddy."

"I love you too, Jon."

It was the last football game we'd ever get to see together.

12

"HE ALWAYS BOUNCED BACK."

No matter what happened to Dean, he always bounced back.

As a child, he broke his wrist while attempting to roller skate (his injury is why I never skated either). As his wrist healed and swelling reduced beneath his cast, Dean realized—to my parents' obvious disapproval—he could slip his entire hand out of his cast and resume his normal activities.

Dean also battled respiratory issues his entire life. He would feel fine one night, then wake up the next morning coughing up blood and immediately going to the hospital. This happened so frequently that his immune system weakened to the point of needing monthly immunoglobulin infusions to stay healthy.

He also had an enlarged heart, a condition called hypertrophic cardiomyopathy. It's the same condition I was diagnosed with at age 13, and the reason I have a small defibrillator implanted inside my chest. When Dean got one too, I joked with him that he didn't have to do *everything* that I did.

Regardless of the injury or illness, Dean was perpetually optimistic. If you asked him how he was feeling, he might give you a little forced cough before saying, "I fine." But he would then smile and talk about all the things he was going to do when he got better.

And without fail, Dean always recovered. Quickly, too.

He logged about a dozen hospital stays with pneumonia, each of which lasted less than a week. After he started receiving his immunoglobulin treatments, he never had to return to the hospital for pneumonia. At most, his pulmonologist would fill an antibiotic prescription, Dean would sleep heavily one day, and then be back to his normal, energetic self the next.

He was Superman.

That's why it scared me so much when, the day after the Super Bowl, Dean woke up coughing up more blood than I had ever seen him cough up before.

Like I said, I did everything possible to keep him out of the Minnesota cold, fearing that the dry, frigid air, would assault his lungs. We spent all but a couple of minutes of that weekend either inside or directly next to a space heater. But what began to unfold that weekend was much bigger than anything we could control.

I rubbed Dean's back as he stood hunched over the hotel toilet. Large streaks of red blood floated in the water below. He began to sob.

"Dean, it's going to be okay. You're going to be okay. You're tough, you're brave, and you've done this before. You'll get better, buddy, I promise."

"Jon," he said in between cries, "I don't want to miss Night to Shine."

That was Dean in a nutshell. Here I was, trying to put together a game plan to get Dean antibiotics, fluids, and rest. Not to mention how we were going to get him well enough to fly home that evening. And Dean was worried about whether or not he was going to get to go to the special-needs prom that was being held the following weekend. I decided to use that as motivation for him.

"Okay, Dean. We'll get you well enough to go dance at Night to Shine. I promise."

"You promise?"

"I promise, Dean. Now let's get you some water."

While Dean settled down and began drinking water, I called my mom to update her on the situation and to see if we could get his antibiotics from a pharmacy in Minneapolis. This process wasn't new for us; it was just the first time we had to do it from different time zones. But within an hour, I was able to give Dean his antibiotics, more fluids, and a little bit of food. I told him to rest, so he slept until four o'clock that afternoon.

When Dean woke up, he seemed completely fine.

"Jon, what we having to eat?"

There's my brother.

He got out of bed and immediately began talking about any and everything. His cough was gone, his breathing was fine, and he had no signs of a fever. Just like Clark Kent stepping out of the phone booth as Superman, Dean got out of bed as the superhero I always knew him to be.

We got home safely later that night, Dean rested and completed his antibiotics, and he was well enough to attend Night to Shine the next weekend. And judging by his spirited rendition of "ABC" by The Jackson 5 in the Karaoke Room of that night's prom, you would never have known that Dean was ever as sick as he was.

But I couldn't shake what I saw him go through that Monday morning following the Super Bowl. I knew something was going on. My mom, a lifelong nurse, had an inkling that something deeper had been developing in Dean's system for months prior to that incident. She had taken him to multiple doctor's appointments and had several blood tests run, but the only thing that came up was that he had a consistently low blood platelet count.

Dean was eventually diagnosed with a condition called Immune thrombocytopenia, or ITP, which meant that he was more susceptible to bruising and bleeding because of his low platelet counts. Platelets help your blood to clot, which is the body's natural response to stop any bleeding. It became apparent that the blood we saw the morning after the Super Bowl may have been related to low platelets.

This diagnosis didn't mean Dean was actively sick, but it was something to monitor. For reference, doctors told us that a "normal" platelet count is around 150, but Dean's normal hovered around 50-75. If his platelets ever bottomed-out completely, he would be more at-risk for other complications.

Dean thought nothing of it—he continued singing and dancing every day, stopping just long enough to finish vacuuming the house and folding the laundry before my parents got home.

He had just finished doing that on Friday, July 27, 2018, and was starting to play a game of NBA 2K18 on his PlayStation when my mom got home from work.

Per daily tradition, Dean paused his game and ran down the hallway to give my mom a big hug to welcome her home.

"Hi mom! I did do my chores today," he said, leaving out the part that he most likely finished them five minutes before she arrived.

"Dean, do you feel okay?" My mom asked.

"I fine, Mom, why?" Dean replied.

My mom noticed small, round, purple spots peppered

across Dean's forehead and down his arms. She knew immediately what was happening. These spots were petechiae, little pockets of blood beneath the skin. Dean's platelets were low.

"Dean, go turn off your game. We need to go to the doctor."

"Mom, I fine!"

"Dean, we need to go to the doctor."

Dean did as he was told—he saved his game of NBA 2K, turned off the PlayStation, put on his shoes, and headed to the car.

Around this time, I got a call from my mom telling me what was going on. We had dinner plans with a couple of our friends, so I called to cancel and Bekah and I drove straight to the emergency room at CMC Pineville to meet my family.

Just hours earlier, I was on my phone, fighting fast-fingered fans to buy tickets to the upcoming Carolina Panthers Fan Fest, the annual event at Bank of America Stadium where fans watch the team practice, sign autographs, and enjoy a fireworks display ahead of the start of the NFL season. I bought tickets on the front row, right next to the tunnel leading to the locker room—prime autograph-seeking position. Dean had been calling me every day for a week talking about wanting to go to Fan Fest. He couldn't wait for the season to start, and he wanted to see his "buddy" Greg Olsen to thank him for the Super Bowl tickets. I knew he would love everything about the experience, so I planned to surprise him with his Fan Fest tickets at the hospital.

When I saw Dean, he was sitting up on a gurney with an IV drip connected to his arm. He was telling his nurse that he got to go to the Super Bowl that February. "My first time going to the Super Bowl," is how he would describe it, believing of course that he would be going again whenever the Panthers made it.

"Sup, Jon! Hi Bekah!" Dean greeted us. "I doing fine!"

We took turns giving him hugs and telling him that we're glad he's doing okay.

"Dean, guess what?" I asked. "We're going to Fan Fest next week."

"Aw, cool! Thanks Jon! Where we sitting? Down low or up high?"

Typical. Dean was no stranger to guilt-tripping me for buying the upper-level tickets.

"Very low, Dean. How does the front row sound?"

"Alright! That's awesome!"

Surprise accomplished.

A few minutes later, a doctor came in to update us that Dean's platelet counts were essentially zero, and that they would need to admit him to a room so he could stay overnight. They would give him platelets through an IV and see how his body responded.

Dean looked dejected. "I be out for Fan Fest next week? I going to Fan Fest next week."

The doctor smiled at Dean, "I can't promise you anything, but we'll do everything we can."

That was enough for Dean. He nodded his head.

As we waited for arrangements to be made to transfer Dean to a hospital room, my family went straight into the logistics of his stay. I would go home and pack a bag for both Dean and my dad. He would stay with Dean and sleep on the guest recliner in his room, and my mom would go home to sleep for the night. If Dean had to stay longer than a night, we would figure things out from there.

But, in that moment, none of us expected him to be there longer than 24-48 hours. I took a picture with Dean before Bekah and I left the emergency room. We both gave a thumbs-up and I laughed as Dean gave a goofy smile.

Dean's platelet count would surely bounce back, and so would he. He always did.

13

"WE'RE GOING TO FIGHT."

The first two nights in the hospital were no different than any stint Dean had endured before.

Our family took turns hanging out in the room with Dean, watching movies on the television in his room. I watched both Jumanji and Jurassic World with Dean, being sure to point out all the places in Hawaii that Bekah and I had visited just a few months earlier. Dean asked a few questions about what Hawaii was like, then we both took turns reminiscing on Dwayne "The Rock" Johnson's days as a WWE wrestler. Dean made sure to point out that he also played football for "The U" in Miami, Florida, just like Dean's "buddy" Greg Olsen.

By Sunday, his platelet count had not risen much, despite the multiple IV drips. His levels would raise from zero to three or four, but drop back to nothing by the next test. That evening, Dean started having respiratory issues. A small cough turned into his oxygen levels dropping. As the doctor's attention shifted towards his breathing, the decision was made to move Dean into the Intensive Care Unit.

Dean's biggest concern? The meal cart was late with his dinner—a cheeseburger with a piece of chocolate cake for dessert—and he was moved to the ICU before he had a chance to eat. Once in the ICU, food wasn't allowed in the rooms, which meant Dean would not get to eat. He lamented this restriction briefly before saying, "That's okay. Dad, I want you to have my cake for dessert."

The ICU only allowed two visitors at a time, and depending on who was volunteering at the check-in desk (a rotation of retirees covered these duties, and we affectionately nicknamed one lady, "The Warden"), you would not be allowed back in the room until the exact moment the designated visiting hours began.

I stayed as late as I could that evening. I brought a stack of four-by-six photos to decorate Dean's room with, as well as his beloved "Keep Pounding" Carolina Panthers towel gifted to him the day Greg Olsen surprised him with Super Bowl tickets.

If there's anything we learned from all of those hospital trips over the years, it was to make Dean—and ourselves—as comfortable as we could be in that hospital room.

My dad and I agreed to rotate the overnight stays with each other throughout the week. He would take this first Sunday night shift so that Bekah and I could sleep at home before going back to work in the morning.

Bekah and I said our goodbyes and told Dean that we would be back the next afternoon. As I left, I started what would become a ritual for each night that I was not staying with him:

"Dean, you going to have a good night tonight?" I asked.

Dean shook his head and said, "Yes, Jon."

"You going to have a good day tomorrow?"

"Yes, Jon."

"You going to be strong and brave for me?"

"Yes I am."

"Alright Dean, I love you. I'll see you tomorrow."

"Hey, Jon."

"Yes, Dean?"

"Ice up, son."

To fully appreciate this moment, you may need to go online and search, "Steve Smith Ice Up Son," and watch what I believe is the best post-game interview in Carolina Panthers' history.

That exchange embodied Dean's attitude in the hospital. He was brave. He was strong. He was positive. And he was fun.

Dean said, "Thank you," to each of his nurses and respiratory therapists who came in-and-out of his room with various treatments. He smiled, chatted, and laughed with anyone who would listen, and not once complained about being stuck in a hospital room.

He knew that this was the same ICU I was in after my sudden cardiac arrest in 2016, and he kept telling me, "Brothers always do things together."

In no time, he had won over each person working in the CMC Pineville ICU.

That first night in the ICU, he would have to rely on the strength of every one of them.

Dean's respiratory issues caused his oxygen saturation levels (a percentage from 1 to 100, with 100 being full capacity) to drop to the point where he needed a special breathing treatment to try to break up the mucus in his lungs and free his airways.

In the process, Dean's lungs started bleeding. With his platelets still at zero, Dean's body had no way to effectively stop the bleeding.

In the wee hours of Monday morning, Dean's lungs were beginning to bleed and he couldn't breathe. Fear gripped him and washed across his face in a way my Dad had never seen before. The Respiratory Therapist forced a breathing tube down Dean's throat and started a ventilator to help him breathe. Scared and in pain, Dean started waving his left hand dramatically, pointing his index finger across the room.

Following his pointing, my Dad saw the "Keep Pounding" towel hanging off of the dresser in the corner of the room.

"Do you want your towel?" My dad asked him.

Dean frantically shook his head up-and-down.

My dad took the towel and laid it across Dean's lap.

"Keep Pounding" became a rally cry for the Carolina Panthers in 2003, when former player and then-coach Sam Mills was diagnosed with cancer. He addressed the team during their run to the Super Bowl and gave them a speech about what it meant to be a Panther. He ended the speech with the phrase, "Keep Pounding," a reminder to never quit, no matter what obstacle or adversity you may be facing.

Dean gripped the towel tightly with his left hand. By morning, Dean had calmed down, grown accustomed to having a breathing tube down his throat, and was finally resting.

Word got to us early Monday morning, so Bekah and I bypassed work and rushed to the hospital. We headed upstairs to the ICU waiting room, where my mom met us by throwing her arms around me and resting her head on my chest, tears wetting the front of my shirt.

"I don't want to lose him," she cried.

A doctor whisked our family into a small room a few steps past the main waiting area. A handful of armchairs sat in a circle, with tissue boxes sitting on end tables in between each chair. It didn't take long to realize that this was the room you see in the movies and TV shows. This is where doctors take families to deliver the kind of news you need to be sitting down for.

"Dean's lungs are hemorrhaging. They are full of blood and we haven't been able to stop the bleeding. The only treatments we have left to stop it may take days or even a week to work, but if this bleeding doesn't stop, Dean may only have a few hours left to live."

"What does that mean? What's next?" I don't remember who asked.

"It means we need to decide whether we want to fight or whether we want to make Dean comfortable. We can be aggressive and I believe we can stop the bleeding, but there's a risk that it either won't work or that it could cause further complications. We already have an experimental drug ordered from CMC Main that is typically used in the field by the military to stop bleeding during emergencies. That is a last resort that we will only use if we have to, but if you want to fight, we can fight."

I looked over at my dad. I had never seen him cry a single time in my entire life, but now tears filled his eyes. I turned to my mom. Tears filled her eyes as she sat with one arm folded and one hand over her mouth. We were all in shock at how serious the situation suddenly was.

This was Dean. He was Superman. He always bounced back from anything he faced. This wasn't supposed to happen like this. We were supposed to go to Fan Fest on Friday. What were we going to do?

I felt a supernatural swell of courage in my chest. Through the tears in all of our eyes, I could see that we were all on the same page.

"We're going to fight. If it's the last time we get to fight for him, so be it. But let's give it everything we can."

"Okay," the doctor said. "We'll get started."

The next hour or so was a blur. I can't remember exactly what treatments they started with, or even if one of my parents went back to Dean's room to be with him.

I sat in a chair in that ICU waiting room, my head buzzing from what I just heard. I stared at the floor. I prayed with words that could only have come from my heart, as my brain was frozen with shock.

"God, this is the same ICU where you performed a miracle through some of these very same doctors and nurses to save my life. Please, God, please save my brother's life. His heart is so pure and his life is so special. Please don't let this be it."

At some point, a nurse pressed the button to swing open the double doors leading from the waiting room into the ICU itself and motioned for our family to come back. We looked at each other, as if to silently figure out which two were going to go back, per ICU rules. The nurse shook her head and said, "No, all of you can come back. He's stable right now. The bleeding is slowing down."

My eyes burned as we walked the twenty yards or so between those doors and room 2323, where Dean was waiting.

What were we about to see? I didn't want to see my hero attached to a breathing machine. I didn't want to see him defeated. I never knew Dean to be discouraged.

I looked to my mom, dad, and my wife Bekah. "Guys, let's be strong for Dean. He always looks to us for assurance when he's scared or nervous. Let's make a deal—we're going to be nothing but positive and strong for him. Even if this is the last time, we're fighting for him every second we're in that room."

"We can do this," my dad said.

As we walked in the room, my mom was first to greet him. "Hey Dean, it's us. How are you?"

His eyes lit up. He couldn't speak due to the breathing tube, but he was there. He smiled. We each took turns coming to his bedside, holding his hand, and talking to him. We asked him questions, and he shook his head "Yes" and "No" in response.

Dean was still with us. The few hours he had left to fight turned into another month that we got to spend with my brother. It was a month that I'll cherish for the rest of my life.

14

BROTHERS FOREVER

I never had any doubt that Dean would make it out of
that hospital.

In hindsight, I don't know if I was ignoring the reality of
the situation, choosing to see the positive in order to stay
strong, or some sort of combination of the two. But it
didn't matter. My goal—and my entire family's goal—
was to be there for Dean.

Dean was in the ICU for just under a month. That
month, contrary to what it may have looked like on the
surface, was one of the best months in any of our lives.
It brought us closer to each other, taught us how to slow
down and be present in the moment, and gave us a
lifetime of little memories to reminisce upon.

Dean was intubated—that is, breathing using a ventilator
and a breathing tube—and unable to talk for at least half
of the time he was in the ICU. It was unusual to be

around Dean in a quiet moment, as he was always the first to speak up and the last to leave any social situation. Personally, with the medication they had Dean on, I wasn't sure how aware he was of his surroundings, or if he would be able to remember what was going on around him.

Still, we took time to talk to him, ask him questions that he could either nod or squeeze a hand in response to, and I made sure to update him on the news surrounding the Carolina Panthers. Specifically, I let Dean know that former Carolina Panther Kelvin Benjamin had just publicly blasted Cam Newton, his former quarterback and one of Dean's favorite players, saying that his career would have been better off with any other quarterback in the league. When I said that, Dean turned his head and stared straight into my eyes. I could tell he wanted to go off on Kelvin Benjamin so badly.

Even though he couldn't speak while intubated, Dean found ways to be flirty with a few of the female nurses. By now you know that Dean was never shy, nor was he ever going to pass on the opportunity to wink at a pretty girl.

This is the same Dean that spent months practicing and improving his bowling score into the mid-100s in preparation for the Special Olympics State Games, only to get a cute 20-something female volunteer as his "buddy" for State Games, which caused him to suddenly "forget" how to bowl. She was none the wiser, and spent the entire day holding his hand and showing him how to roll the ball. Dean's score that day? Forty-nine.

Enter Jessica, one of Dean's nurses in the ICU. She is an incredible nurse who takes incredible care of her patients, but also takes the time to get to know each patient and his or her family. Granted, I only saw her interact with Dean. But her upbeat, joyful, and sincere personality makes it a safe bet to believe she was a favorite nurse for almost any patient on that floor. She was Dean's favorite, that's for sure (I'm sure the pretty smile and the long, blonde hair influenced Dean's opinion some, too).

Every time Jessica came into the room, Dean perked up. He sat up a little straighter in his bed. His eyes opened a little wider. He was much more emphatic and cooperative in whatever exercises she gave him to do.

Once, after Dean had been in the ICU for long enough to cause his muscles to atrophy, Jessica attempted to reposition Dean in his bed. She leaned over him, almost face-to-face, and said, "Dean, I'm going to reach around you to pick you up. I need you to put your arms around me like you're giving me a big hug, okay?"

Dean turned his head and looked directly at my dad. He grinned from ear-to-ear.

Whenever Jessica asked Dean to do anything, he would happily follow her orders. After we told Jessica that Dean had a little crush on her, she asked, "Dean, are you a ladies' man?"

Dean nodded, then started quickly lifting his eyebrows up-and-down.

Needless to say, if we had any difficulty whatsoever with Dean during his time in the ICU, Jessica could bring his playful personality back to life.

Under her care (and many other incredible nurses and respiratory therapists), his breathing began to drastically improve. They had already attempted to remove Dean's breathing tube once, but much to our chagrin, the bleeding in his lungs began again and Dean had to be re-intubated. But this time, his platelet count was climbing higher and higher. We went from celebrating platelet counts of 6, 8, and 10, to hearing numbers between 20 and 40. Dean's breathing improved to the point where his respiratory therapists were essentially turning the ventilator off for short periods of time to see how well Dean's lungs could operate on their own. Through it all, his oxygen levels stayed strong.

All the while, we were in Dean's ear, coaching him up as if he was Rocky Balboa on the verge of beating Drago. "Dean, you got this, buddy! You're so strong! Look at those numbers, Dean! Look at you go!"

We could see the finish line for Dean's ventilator coming closer and closer. Jessica called into work and picked up an extra shift just to be there the day that Dean's tube came out.

When the time came to leave the ventilator behind for good, we were all nervous. Our family sat in the waiting room, holding our breath for what felt like an hour. Finally, Jessica came back and told us to come see Dean—he was doing great!

When we walked into the room, Dean was talking faster than a Lamborghini sports car.

I had stayed overnight with Dean the night before, and we had watched the Panthers win a preseason game on the hospital room television. When I asked Dean if he remembered watching the game with me, he didn't answer me with a "Yes" or "No". He started singing:

"Sweeeeet Caroline, bum bum bummm…"

The traditional victory song for the Panthers sounded a little more nasally than usual, as Dean now had pressurized oxygen flowing through his nose. It didn't slow him down.

"Good times never seemed so good… So good! So good! So good!"

Dean started coughing, presumably from the mucus moving around from just having a breathing tube removed.

"Hey Jessica!" Dean called out to his favorite nurse. He cleared his throat.

"Yes, Dean?" She asked. "It's so good to hear your voice!"

Dean started lifting his eyebrows up-and-down again, just like he had done for the last few days.

"That was for you," Dean said. Dean "The Ladies Man" was back.

"Alright, Dean. Let's settle down for a little while," we told him.

"Hold on, hold on!" Dean interrupted. "One thing. Kelvin Benjamin…"

Oh my goodness, he remembered what I told him!

"Kelvin Benjamin, I so glad you gone. Bye bye, Benjamin! Bye bye!"

The room erupted in laughter. We were told that it usually took a while for people to get their energy and their voice back after being intubated for that long. Dean was singing, talking, and cracking jokes within minutes.

Dean turned to me and said, "Jon, since we not go to Fan Fest, how 'bout you take me to a game instead?"

"Sure thing Dean. You got it. But tickets are expensive. Is the preseason okay?"

"No, Jon. Preseason sucks."

Point made. I went out and bought four tickets to the Panthers and Ravens game on October 28, a week after Dean's and the actual day of my mom's birthday. He always knew how to get to me.

For a few blissful days afterwards, Dean seemed to mostly make progress in his recovery. His breathing improved. There was no sign of any kind of internal bleeding. His biggest challenge was now managing the balancing act that was his blood pressure and how his body retained fluid. Doctors aggressively treated the hemorrhaging in his lungs in the previous weeks, so these all seemed to be the kinds of complications we knew we were risking by pushing to save his life that day.

As a family, our focus shifted towards getting Dean well enough to leave the ICU and move into a rehabilitation program, where he could regain enough strength to move around, walk, and one day resume life's normal activities.

Dean's spirits began to improve too, and going into the last weekend in August, he was doing so well that we invited his friends to come see him and hang out in the hospital. A few had already visited, but we kept the masses at bay—I use that word intentionally; Dean had a lot of friends—because we didn't know how some of them might handle seeing him in the hospital hooked up to so many machines. By this point, however, Dean had transitioned off of the pressurized oxygen that constantly pushed air down his nasal passages and onto a much more subdued and "regular" oxygen treatment.

That weekend, one by one, Dean's friends came to see him. Justin. Ben. Cat. Robin. Caleb. Each of the coaches from the inaugural season of Challenger Flag Football came to visit Dean. They even brought him a gift basket with a brand-new coach's visor, with the Panthers' logo emblazoned on the front. Even Mark, one of his overnight nurses gifted Dean a brand-new Panthers blanket and offered to let him use his season tickets to attend a game. Several of my friends came to visit as well, although this is where Dean would correct me and say, "They my friends too, Jon."

Dean smiled and laughed with each person who came in. As each of them left to go home, Dean made sure to say the same thing to all of his friends:

"I love you."

It's hard to put into words what happened after that weekend. We were all on such an emotional high from seeing Dean improve that it didn't seem real when his body began to shut down.

That Sunday night, when his body stopped responding to the medicines meant to remove excess fluids, or his liver functions started dipping, we hoped these would just be small hiccups.

We just took two big steps forward, so what's one small step back? At least that's how I saw it at the time.

In hindsight, I believe there was a special kind of grace in what would become Dean's final weekend. Dean seemed entirely himself and offered such sweet, loving goodbyes to each of his friends. I believe that those days were a little gift from God, a way of giving Dean a chance to say goodbye to the people he loved the most.

That Monday morning, things took a sudden turn for the worst. Long story short, and because I'm not able to fully understand the medical specifics of the situation, Dean's organs simply couldn't take it anymore. Between all the trauma his body went through and all of the medication and treatment to attempt to bring him back to health, things began to shut down. He wasn't able to naturally remove excess fluid, which put pressure on his heart and lungs, which was exacerbated by his pre-existing heart condition, and ultimately made it difficult for Dean to breathe. He wasn't stable enough to undergo surgery, and doctors had essentially run out of treatment options.

This time, when they took our family into that same dreadful conference room, they told us that there was nothing left to fight anymore. It was only a matter of time before Dean was no longer with us.

Representatives from Hospice, as well as other hospital support staff, met with us to let us know that they were going to do everything they could to make Dean's final hours as comfortable and as pain-free as possible. They did just that.

All day long, I felt like I was in a free-fall. I could feel myself floating, trying to be strong for my family, trying to stay positive and present with my brother, but I felt like I was never going to land.

We told our immediate family and a few of our closest friends what was going on, and a number of them showed up at the hospital that day to see him. I'm forever grateful for each of those people—if you're reading this, you know who you are. You held my family up that day.

The last ones to visit were my best friends Matt and Christina, a couple I grew up with, and who got married after being high school sweethearts. Both of them loved

Dean, and Dean loved them like a brother and a sister. By this point, Dean wasn't responding. He looked to already be in a peaceful sleep. Matt prayed with Dean, gave him a hug, and told him that he loved him.

After walking Matt and Christina out of the room, my family—my mom, dad, Bekah, and I—were the only ones left. We had no idea how long it would be, but we decided to all stay by Dean's side until he passed.

Bekah went downstairs to the cafeteria to buy snacks for all of us, as I don't believe any of us had eaten dinner. When she got back, I happened to look up at the monitor above Dean's bed, the same monitor that had told us his heart rate, blood pressure, and oxygen levels for the last month. It was now silenced and blacked out, but had an alert symbol flashing in the corner of the screen. I could hear the faint sound of beeping at the nurse's station down the hall, which seemed to confirm what I was seeing on the monitor.

"Guys, it's happening."

Everyone dropped what they were doing and surrounded Dean's bed. One by one, we all took our turn telling Dean that we loved him one last time. We all gave him a hug, and even though he couldn't hug us back, we knew that he felt it.

I was holding his left hand when I leaned down and whispered in his ear the words I was never going to be ready to say:

"Dean, it's okay. Jesus is ready for you now. You can go

to him. I'm going to miss you, but I know you're going to be okay. I love you, Dean. We're brothers forever."

With that, I felt Dean take his last breath.

At 10:35 p.m. on Monday, August 27, 2018, my brother Dean Adcock went to Heaven. He was 33 years old.

15

"JON, WHY GOD MAKE

ME DIFFERENT?"

One night when I was in high school, I was walking past Dean's room and noticed he looked upset. Anytime he was in his room and there was no music, dancing, or video games, something was up.

"Dean, you okay?" I stopped to ask him.

With tears welling up in his eyes, he turned to me, "Jon, why God make me different?"

I was floored. My brother was an eternal optimist and the biggest source of joy in my life, and in many others' as well. But he wasn't ignorant; he knew he was different than most people. He never dwelled on it, but he would occasionally point out some of the things he couldn't or wouldn't get to do because he had Down syndrome.

Some things he accepted, like driving a car. He never had much desire to do that. Other things, like when I moved away from home to go to college, bothered him more. Dean spent a few months where he didn't understand why he couldn't move away and have his own place. Once we compared how much money rent cost per month with how much cash was in his wallet at that moment in time, he stopped worrying about having his own place.

For the most part, however, these conversations were pretty circumstantial. He might see someone doing something and wonder if or when he could do that, but he never dug beneath the surface to make it personal. It always involved what he could or couldn't do. Not once had he ever asked me anything about who he was. That's what struck me to my core.

"Jon, why God make me different?" It echoed in my brain.

I took a deep breath and sat down next to him on his bed.

I told him, "Yeah man, God did make you different. He made you better than any of us."

Dean looked up at me, hanging onto my words and trying his best to fully comprehend.

"Everyone loves you, Dean."

He smiled and chuckled, as if to say, "Yeah, I know."

"Listen. You make everyone around you better just because of who you are. That's a good reason to be different."

He never asked me that question again.

Now, I can't say whether or not he truly understood what I was trying to tell him. He simply gave me a big hug and told me, "I love you, Jon," before we turned on the PlayStation and played against each other in an NCAA football video game.

But I never forgot that question. It would pop into my mind as I tried to fall asleep at night, or occasionally it would cross my mind as I stared ahead at the highway on a long drive.

"Why God make me different?"

A pit would form in my stomach, as it pained me to believe that someone as truly special as Dean ever had doubts about who he was. I guess we all do.

But it made me smile too. I couldn't help but appreciate Dean's sincerity in asking that question. It's how he lived his life—everything was real, authentic, and true. Dean had the purest heart of anyone I've ever met. I know that regardless of how many times he may have asked himself that question, he never let doubt stop him from being uniquely Dean.

I think that's what I miss the most. All the little ways that Dean was just, well... Dean.

Working for a church, Friday is traditionally our day off. So I started a tradition where I would come over to my parents' house every Friday to pick Dean up and take him to lunch.

While my parents worked, Dean would have the house to himself. And without fail, every single Friday, I'd unlock the door and walk in to Dean dancing his heart out in front of the living room TV.

Most days, he would have on either VH1, BET, or MTV—whichever channel was showing music videos that hour—and he would mimic the moves he saw the dancers executing in each video. Later, I would gift him my iPad and show him how to use YouTube, which only took his self-guided dance lessons to new levels of awesome.

I miss walking into the kitchen and dining room area, where Dean would have an assortment of spiral-bound notebooks scattered across the table. He was constantly writing lists—favorite songs, favorite dancers, best love songs, and so on. He would copy word-for-word excerpts from the sports section of The Charlotte Observer and write out his predictions for the upcoming Carolina Panthers and Charlotte Hornets seasons. When he learned how to use Google, he would research NFL mock drafts every Spring and write out his own projections. More often than not, he was spot-on with those.

I miss laughing at the way he would scramble to complete his household chores just before my parents returned home from work. Dancing, singing, and studying the latest sports news could really cause the day to slip away from him.

I miss his daily phone calls. Sometimes, he'd call multiple times a day, even if I was at work. I would always feel guilty when I didn't answer, but I'm so glad I saved all of his voicemails. Each one started the exact same way:

"Hey Jon! I just call to say I love you..."

Then came what I termed, "The Roll Call":

"How Bekah doing? How her sister Sam doing? How Kait doing? How Biggie (Bekah and my pug) doing?"

If I answered, I would sometimes cut him off and list them myself, "Bekah's fine, Biggie's fine, Sam's fine, Kait's fine too."

"Huh! That's good!" He would chuckle.

Then, depending on the time of year, Dean would launch into any pertinent life updates that I needed to know about. It typically revolved around upcoming birthdays—he had every birthday in the family written down on a piece of paper that he kept on his nightstand—or if something important was happening with one of his favorite sports teams.

"Jon, who the Panthers going to draft this year? What you think?"

"Dean, it's January. This season's not even over and the draft is over three months away. I have no idea."

"I just asking, Jon. I just thinking about it."

"Well, who do you think? You know more about this stuff than I do."

For at least three years in a row, Dean was correct on who the Panthers would draft. He knew what he was talking about.

I miss how Dean would try to get me to take him to games. He made sure to tell me which games were happening around his birthday in October, as well as what was happening around Christmas.

"Are you trying to get me to take you to one of those games, Dean?"

"I just telling you, Jon. I just telling you."

Uh-huh. Sure.

One time, Dean went as far as to offer to pay for the tickets himself. The only problem was his inability to comprehend the value of those tickets.

"Jon, how much tickets cost? I buy them."

"I'm not sure, Dean. Maybe $100 each?"

Dean dug his wallet out of his pocket and thumbed through his cash. He shook his head.

"Here, Jon," he handed me all the money in his wallet.

"Just take it."

He had thirty dollars.

I miss how he had no problem resorting to guilt-tripping me to get what he wanted.

While home from college break, my friends and I would head out in the wee hours of the morning to go to Taco Bell, several hours after Dean was supposed to be in bed, asleep.

Then his bedroom door would crack and he would be walking to the kitchen because he was "thirsty." Then, as we were about to walk out the door, he'd hit us with the, "Man, I love Taco Bell!"

Or if I surprised him with tickets to that night's Charlotte Hornets game, as he got in the car, he would ask, "Jon, we sitting down low? Good seats?"

"Dean, we're in the upper level. But they're still good seats."

"That's okay, Jon. I still love you."

I'm telling you, Dean was a professional.

I miss the sincere, unassuming view he had on life.

I miss how Dean would correct us if we said that we hated something. "Hate is not good," he would say.

My friend Matt is a big Miami Dolphins fan, and as he

lamented the New England Patriots one day, Dean heard him say, "I hate Tom Brady."

"No, Matt. Don't hate anybody, not even Tom Brady."

I miss how much he loved to say the blessing before a meal with our family.

I miss how we always had to remind him, "Dean, it's a blessing, not a sermon."

"Okay, I do know that," he would answer.

Almost five full minutes later, Dean was still thanking God for both the dinner rolls and the way he delivered David from Goliath.

I miss the way he would latch onto music biopics and obsess over movies like, "The Jackson Five: The American Dream," "Jersey Boys," "The Temptations", and "La Bamba."

I miss the way he would get into my car and ask, "Jon, you got any 'Fitty Cent' CDs in here?"

There truly was no one like Dean.

I'm forever grateful for that. He saw the best in people. He found joy in the smallest things. And he was grateful for anything and anyone he ever encountered. It's rare to find someone like that in a world that is always pushing for more—more money, more possessions, more status, more recognition, or sometimes just more time.

He was just different. In the best possible way.

Grief is a fickle beast; it can both blindside you with indescribable pain, as well as gently comfort you with a familiar memory. I've learned in these early days of grieving that it's best not to run from these moments, but to let them hit me so that I can extract from grief the memories I need to move forward.

Dean's memory has changed the way I'll see life. Forever. And I believe his legacy will be how his life changes the way you see yours.

16

DARE TO LIVE LIKE DEAN

The days following Dean's passing were tough, to say the least.

I remember collapsing on the floor just inside the front door immediately after returning home from the hospital. I remember the physical pain that I felt in my chest that night as I tried to sleep. I remember thinking, "This must be what heartbreak feels like."

I remember crying out to God, "Why didn't you save Dean? Why didn't you save Dean like you saved me?"

I remember crying out to Dean, "I'm so sorry, buddy. I'm so sorry. I told you it was going to be okay."

I remember wishing I could have taken his place on that hospital bed. I remember wishing I could give any and everything to have him back. I remember missing the sounds of the ICU. I never thought I'd say this, but I remember even wishing I could sleep on that broken hospital-room recliner that I was at least six inches too tall for.

But in the midst of all the grief and sadness, the thing I remember the most is that all of us—everyone in our family—kept finding peace in knowing that Dean was okay now. His fight was over. He wasn't sick anymore. He wasn't in the hospital anymore. I believe He is in Heaven, where he wouldn't be limited by anything in this world ever again.

I don't know what your thoughts are on life after death, but I do know that one of the most-asked questions in the world is, "What happens after all of this?"

I don't have a definitive answer. I've never been on the other side of this life, even if my enlarged heart has gotten me close a few times. And though I can't say with confidence if there's a connection between those who are here on Earth and those who have passed on, I've personally had a few moments where the veil between the two seemed almost thin enough to see through.

I call it my own, personal "Butterfly Effect".

When I woke up on Tuesday morning, the day after Dean passed away, I was dreading what was sure to be an endless stream of family and friends coming in-and-out of my parent's house. I just wasn't in any kind of mood to socialize with anyone at all.

But as I walked up the steps to my parents' house, I saw something I had never seen in the nearly fourteen years that they had lived in that house:

A black and Carolina-blue butterfly. We rarely, if ever had any butterflies in the yard. We had no bushes or trees for them to rest upon. But yet, here fluttered a butterfly whose wings were adorned in the signature colors of Dean's beloved Carolina Panthers.

It floated up to me and Bekah, circled us, and landed on the railing just a couple feet from the door. My mom and dad stepped outside to greet us, and the butterfly leapt towards them, circling both my parents as one would when reuniting with a long-lost friend.

As we all marveled at the beauty of this little creature, it fluttered away, zig-zagging the length of the house. Then, as fate would have it, it landed gently on the roof directly above Dean's bedroom. We stood on the steps of the house, all fighting back tears, and watched as the butterfly proudly stretched its wings.

I know this might seem silly to you, but I chose in that moment to believe that this was a little wink from my brother.

One night in the ICU, after having his breathing tube removed, Dean suddenly opened his eyes wide and smiled. His finger lifted into the air and followed something that he saw floating through his hospital room.

"What do you see, Dean?" I asked.

It is common for ICU patients to begin to hallucinate

after being hospitalized for an extended period of time. It's a combination of illness, drugs, and the flat-out mental strain that comes with being confined to a hospital bed. He had a few of these moments, so I was preparing to talk him through it.

"Butterfly!" He exclaimed.

I brushed it off and reminded him that there wasn't anything in the room. I told him that he was dreaming, but that everything was okay.

"No, Jon," he gently corrected me. "Butterfly."

Standing on the steps of my parents' house, watching a very real butterfly land on the roof above his room, gave me all the perspective I needed.

Dean was okay now. And we were going to be okay too.

All day long, everyone who visited said the same thing:

"Did you see that butterfly? It flew right up to me!"

A lot of people might call that coincidence, but this same butterfly circled every single family member and friend who visited us that day. It all happened the same way, too. They would park their car in the driveway, step out, and the butterfly would swirl a foot or two above them, then return to its perch above Dean's bedroom window.

Now, on every big anniversary of something significant in Dean's life—a birthday, the first Camp SOAR since he passed, our first Panthers game without him—a butterfly appears. If only for a moment, we see it.

We chose to see it as a sign. Not just that Dean is okay, but that his spirit and his legacy were alive and well within each of us.

I know that there is something to be said for the fact that if you are subconsciously looking for something, you will inevitably see it. It's a psychological phenomenon that we've all almost surely experienced. For instance, if you're looking at purchasing a Toyota Camry, guess what you're going to see everywhere for the next few days on the road? Toyota Camrys.

Perhaps that's what my family is experiencing. We bonded over seeing this butterfly, so now we're always looking for them. We even planted a butterfly bush beneath Dean's bedroom window, a symbolic reminder of him.

To borrow this concept, I want to challenge you with Dean's story. Look for Dean in the world around you. Look for the joy in life's smallest moments. Look for the good in people. Look for ways to help others. Look for reasons to smile, to laugh, and to dance.

Regardless of what life throws at you, never limit yourself to your abilities or disabilities. Lean on the people closest to you; love them hard. Let people help you when you need it. Push yourself to try new things you've always told yourself you couldn't do.

Dean did it. He did it well.

So let Dean's story continue through you. In the way you treat people and in the way you live your life, dare to do it like Dean.

DREAM BIG.

Dean's favorite way to start any sentence included these three words:

"One day, I…"

This phrase became infamous around our house. We knew that whatever Dean said next would be his next big dream.

The only thing is… Dean actually made a lot of them happen.

Some of them didn't even seem possible. Kind of like:

"One day, I be famous. I be in the newspaper."

Tom Sorenson, Dean's favorite sports columnist, writes a column all about Dean

"Look, Jon! I famous!"

"One day, I be on stage dancing. Just me, dancing by myself."

Dean, at "Night to Shine", solo-dances to Usher in front of hundreds of people

"Go Dean! Go Dean! Go Dean!" The crowd roars.

And, of course, Dean's all-time greatest prediction:

"One day, I go to the Super Bowl, Jon. You not buying tickets. I am."

"Yeah, Dean, that sounds great!"

Fast-forward to February 2018 in Minneapolis, Minnesota

"Jon, we at the Super Bowl! This is awesome!"

"Yes, Dean. Yes it is."

We never outright shut down his dreams to his face. We let him imagine whatever grand ideas he could think of. But out of his earshot, my family would often laugh at the childlike innocence and belief he showed in some of his proclamations.

But Dean's dreams came true so often that we stopped doubting them altogether.

"Who knows?" We would say. "Crazier things have happened."

Dean's story has taught me not to squash my own dreams. Perhaps his life could inspire the same for you.

Your dreams will never have life if you don't breathe life into them. If you don't say it, if you don't dream it, and if you don't give yourself the permission to believe for something unbelievable, that dream you've stored up in your heart will probably never see the light of day.

Dean had plenty of reasons not to dream. He knew he had Down syndrome. He knew he wasn't as tall, strong, fast, or as naturally-talented as most people in the world.

Though Dean was surrounded by amazing people who loved him and pushed him to dream, there were still some people who couldn't look beneath the surface to see his heart.

Once, on a bring-your-child-to-work day, a co-worker asked my dad:

"What's wrong with your son?"

My dad cut them off immediately.

"Not a thing is wrong with him. God made him exactly how he's supposed to be."

You can't allow the voices of your limitations to shout louder than your heart's desires. Sometimes, that voice comes from within. Other times, it comes from the limitations other people place upon us. But even if it takes an army of friends helping you stand up for yourself, you can't allow your own deficiencies to disqualify you from your dreams.

If you want to live like Dean, look your limitations in the eyes and dream big anyway. Remind yourself that no dream is too big or too unattainable. Open your world. Train yourself not just to believe the impossible; but to expect it.

Life can be a lot more fun if you do.

EMBRACE LIMITATIONS.

The danger of dreaming big is painfully obvious:

Your dreams don't always come true.

There were plenty of "One day, I…" statements that never happened for Dean.

Because Dean had Down syndrome, there were some dreams that were simply never going to happen for him.

Did that slow Dean down? Did that stop him from dreaming? Not one bit.

For every dream Dean had, he had another dream. A bigger, wilder, even-more-impossible dream.

And if they didn't happen? Dean had another phrase:

"That's okay!"

Full disclosure: Dean may have intentionally used that phrase to guilt-trip me into taking him places and buying him things. Yet, he changed my outlook on life's challenges through those same words.

If he couldn't do something the way everyone else could, he would say, "That's okay," and find another way.

It never occurred to Dean, like it so often does for me, to get frustrated and pout about it or give up. He just kept trying, even in the smallest of instances.

For example, when he discovered our grandmother's King James Bible, Dean realized that the print was too small and difficult for him to read, even with glasses. What did he do? He used the iPad I had recently given him to take pictures of the pages he wanted to read, just so he could zoom in and make the letters larger.

It was a simple solution, but impressive nonetheless. No one taught Dean how to zoom in using a touch-screen device; he figured out how to do that on his own.

In the same way, Dean navigated many of the obstacles and limitations life would present him by simply forging a new path. His life was filled with ingenious little work-arounds; small ways he could adapt and make the most out of life.

It's really simple, but it's an art form that we all have to master if we're going to find any kind of enjoyment in life.

Sometimes life happens and forces far outside of our own control make things difficult, or sometimes impossible for us to handle. Sometimes, our own mistakes back us into a corner where we feel like we have no way out.

A defeated mindset sees these limitations, stops, and says, "I can't."

A Dean mindset says, "That's okay that I can't _____. I still can ____."

That shift changes everything.

You aren't built to live anyone else's life but your own. Embrace our own limitations as an invitation to forge a path through life that's unique to you.

Many people would look at Dean and feel sorry for him having to live with a disability. But Dean's Down syndrome unlocked his ability to live in a way that I've always envied: With pure joy, love, and contentment.

ACCEPT EVERYONE.

Dean never met someone he didn't love.

Whenever he met new people, he would shake their hand, give them a hug, or just flash a huge smile. He assumed at first-sight that whoever he was meeting was now his friend.

I know that many of us have been jaded by our past relationships. We've all met someone who hurt us when we never believed they would. Because of that, it's hard for a lot of us to let our guards down and trust people like we wish we could. I understand and respect that.

But Dean inherently understood—even though I don't remember our family ever sitting down and having a pointed conversation about this—that it didn't matter how different someone was from him, he was supposed to love them.

One of the most beautiful things about Dean's community was that everyone was vastly different from each other. Everyone in his classes at school, in his groups at Summer Camp, or on his team during Special Olympics, fell in a different place along an impossibly-large spectrum.

Dean was always surrounded by people of different shapes, sizes, genders, ethnicities, religious backgrounds, intellectual abilities, and physical limitations. To Dean, none of that mattered. The only descriptor he would use for each of them was simple:

Friend.

Every person who entered Dean's life stayed as a friend. Whether or not they saw each other every day was irrelevant.

Once you met Dean, you were his friend for life. He accepted everyone for who they were. He never rejected someone for who they weren't, or turned them away for what they couldn't do.

I believe this is one of the most beautiful aspects of the special-needs community. Everyone is so unique in the ways that their minds and bodies and personalities have developed that it's impossible to say two people are exactly alike. That's why they all love each other so much.

If one person can do something special—like Dean's dancing—everyone else celebrates. If one person can't do something that everyone else can—like Dean not being able to tie his shoes—the rest of the group jumps in to help.

That's a beautiful world to be a part of.

That was the world Dean knew. It shaped him. In turn, it shaped me. I'm forever grateful that I was born into it. And if you're reading this, I hope you get to experience—and help to create—this kind of world, too.

NEVER GIVE UP.

I guess every hero needs a hero themselves.

Dean borrowed the "Keep Pounding" mantra of our beloved Carolina Panthers as motivation to keep going when life got tough. The "Cardiac Cats" clad in black-and-blue were his heroes; their persistence on-and-off the field taught him that it takes strength to win, but even more strength to experience defeat and still fight for victory another day.

Dean was only five-foot-three inches tall. He would've looked like a child standing next to some of the giants that line up for the Panthers on a weekly basis. But whether Dean knew it or not, his spirit was even stronger than that of his athletic heroes'.

Over the years, I watched Dean do things that no person with Down syndrome is ever expected to do. I cheered

him on as he competed with all his heart on the
basketball court or football field. I held his hand as he
sat in a hospital bed. And I was with him for everything
in between.

Dean never gave up.

It just wasn't in him to do it.

It wasn't that long ago that it was commonplace for
children born with Down syndrome to be given up by
their families and institutionalized their entire lives. The
world gave up on many people like Dean before they
ever had a chance to become who they were meant to
be.

Dean was fortunate to grow up in an environment that
embraced him, supported him, and gave him the
freedom to be himself. I'm forever grateful for my
parents and the people in Dean's life who allowed Dean
to become the brother that I got to love and learn from.

But Dean's perseverance was something only he could
cultivate. His strength and determination have inspired
me for years. They always will.

Regardless of how many nights Dean had to stay in the
hospital—from his battles with pneumonia to his final
month of life in the ICU—he never complained. He
faced everything with an unshakeable resolve and an
optimism that I've always envied. Even on the day he
passed away, he spent the morning asking to do his arm
exercises so that he could "get better and get out of
here."

I take solace now knowing that Dean is in a better place where he doesn't have to worry about limitations, disabilities, or health issues. I believe Dean is in Heaven, full of joy and peace.

But sometimes—wildly and unexpectedly—grief punches me in the gut and makes me want to give up on everything in front of me. Even though I've overcome a lot of limitations in my own life, I have plenty of days where I find myself too tired to fight. I fall into this self-defeating dialogue of, "I've been through enough as it is. I didn't go through all of that to have to deal with this now. I just want to give up on all of it."

That's when I can hear Dean's voice, as clear as day.

"Don't give up, Jon. I love you, Jon."

That's what gives me the strength to pick myself up and press on. I know that even on my worst days, I'm one day closer to being reunited with my brother.

When Dean passed away, he didn't lose his fight. He won in the way he lived his life each and every day.

So I'm not going to give up on his legacy. And now that you know Dean, neither should you.

Dream big.
Embrace limitations.
Accept everyone.
Never give up.

Let's continue the Dean story. In the way that we live each day. In the way that we treat people. Let's not give up on all the wonder and joy and love that life can bring.

Dean will be proud of us if we do.

EPILOGUE

As Dean's brother, the majority of this book is told through the lens of my own experiences with Dean. I wanted this to feel like you and I were sitting across from each other while I told you about my brother.

I looked up to him in every way except in our height (I'm six-foot-four, Dean was five-foot-three). I always wanted to have him with me, or more likely, me with him, because he made everything so much more joyful.

But so much of life with Dean included so many other incredible people like him. And maybe you'll think this is a strange thought, but growing up, I thought that everyone had someone like Dean in their family. My best friend throughout elementary and middle school had a younger brother with Down syndrome. I spent my weekends volunteering at Special Olympics, where most of the athletes were like Dean, and most of them had brothers and sisters like me.

It wasn't until I got to middle school that I started to see the ugly truth—that many people don't know anyone like Dean. And in fact, many people actually make fun of people like my brother.

I was ready to fight somebody the first time I heard "the r-word" tossed around that middle school lunch room.

Over the years, I watched as Dean's unrivaled social skills transformed so many people's perspectives on people with disabilities. I'm not exaggerating when I say that Dean opened the doors for inclusion everywhere he went.

With a front-row seat to his impact, I always believed that the world would be a much better place if everyone actually did know Dean, or at least someone like him.

That's one of the primary reasons I made myself finish this book. These stories aren't meant just to help me grieve and heal; they're meant to introduce you to Dean and the way he saw the world.

I want you to see that it doesn't matter what your age, gender, race, sexual orientation, or your physical, developmental, or intellectual ability or disability may be. You are a special, unique person worthy of the utmost love and respect.

Dean spent his entire life sharing that kind of pure unconditional love with the world around him.

It's only right that I leave you with love as a central theme.

With that in mind, I want to end this book with an, "I love you," said in true Dean fashion, to the people he loved the most.

So here goes.

Matt Price. Dean's first and best friend. Thank you for always laughing with Dean and putting up with him when his ideas got you both into trouble. Pete and Repeat forever.

Justin Beshears. You are the one Dean could always turn to talk Panthers and country music. If only we could keep you guys from trying to sneak kisses from the pretty ladies at those concerts.

Ben Sansbury. Consistent. Loyal. You two thought the exact same way. You were both girl crazy and always cracked me up with your big plans for "one day in the future…"

Caleb Kelly. From intense video game battles to shooting contests on the basketball court, you and Dean shared the purest of friendships.

Damian Chwalek. Your touchdown dances are unrivaled. Thank you for looking out for Dean and always being there for him. Keep being the fun, strong, and hilarious young man you are.

Robin Calloway. Dean's forever prom date. Thank you for being one of the most thoughtful people we've ever known and one of the best friends Dean ever had. Keep carrying your torch and shining your light everywhere you go.

Cat Spantgos. Dean's kindred spirit. I had never met
anyone quite like Dean until I met you. I know you both
made sure to tell me that you were "just friends," but we
all know you guys had something special.

Dean's classmates. Matt, Dominique, Jeffrey, Kandy,
Tara. All of you. From Devonshire to A.G. to East
Meck, you guys ruled the world. You're some of my
favorite people in the entire world.

Dean's Special Olympics buds. Peter, Sharday, Donald,
Andy, Rayshaun. Keep surprising people with what you
can do. And keep collecting that hardware!

Dean's teachers and coaches. Mrs. Hanson. Bob Bowler.
Coach Fred. Nancy Calloway. Your leadership helped
Dean to grow from "creatively mischievous" to the
leader we all got to know and love over the years.

Riley Fields. You are forever Dean's buddy. Thank you
for getting Dean into the coolest places. You are proof
that an organization as big as yours truly cares about
each individual person. You made Dean feel like a rock
star.

Bekah. The best sister-in-law Dean could ever have.
When you came around, my word ceased existence as
"The Golden Rule" in Dean's life. It became all about
Bekah. He loved you so much.

Mom, Dad. When you found out Dean had Down
syndrome, raising him may have seemed like the biggest

challenge you'd ever face in life. But you made it your greatest calling and your crowning achievement. The impact he's made is a direct result of the way you loved and believed in him.

Dean, I know where you are there's no need for little paperback books. But I know you're proud.

I love you buddy. Brothers forever.

ABOUT THE AUTHOR

Jonathan Adcock was born and raised in Charlotte, North Carolina, where he currently resides with his wife, Bekah, and their pug, Biggie.

Jonathan is borderline obsessive over the Carolina Panthers, Charlotte Hornets, and hip-hop music. He refers to himself as an "Enneagram Five" and is very uncomfortable writing about himself in third-person. But he really doesn't have a choice right now, does he? This is the "About the Author" section, after all.

That being said, this is Jonathan's first—and certainly not his last—book. He'd like to thank you for getting to know his brother Dean through the pages of what he often refers to as, "The Dean Book". Now, if you'll kindly share this book with someone who needs to know Dean, the world would be a much better place.

Have a nice day.

*For more information on this book, or just to watch a video of Dean's sick dance moves, visit **thedeanbook.com**.*

Made in the USA
Columbia, SC
02 November 2019